The Balanced Leader: Creating Sustainable Performance Through Awareness, Alignment, and Presence

By Joy Hafner

Truejoy Publishing

TRUEJOY@WORK

A Year-Long Leadership Transformation

COPYRIGHT PAGE

The Balanced Leader: Creating Sustainable Performance Through Awareness, Alignment, and Presence

Copyright © 2026 by Joy Hafner

Publisher:
TrueJoy Publishing
An imprint of Joy Hafner Inc.

TrueJoy™ are trademarks of Joy Hafner Inc.

ISBN (Paperback): 978-1-971164-24-3
ISBN (Hardcover): 978-1-971164-11-3

First Edition

Printed in the United States of America

TABLE OF CONTENTS

Introduction

Why Leadership Needs a New Model

PART I — THE MODERN LEADERSHIP CHALLENGE

PART II — THE BALANCED LEADER FRAMEWORK

PART III — CULTURE & COLLECTIVE IMPACT

PART IV — EMBODIMENT & LEADERSHIP PRESENCE

PART V — LEGACY & TRANSFORMATION

Appendix

Workbook & Leadership Integration Pages

Introduction

Why Leadership Needs a New Model

Leadership is changing fast. The modern leader is measured by far more than simple productivity. You're now expected to drive performance, care for your people, shape culture, and ensure long-term sustainability—all at the same time.

For decades, the standard playbook for leadership rested on one core idea: push harder, get more. More effort, more urgency, more output. And for a while, that approach delivered. But the landscape is fundamentally different now. The contemporary workplace is characterized by unrelenting communication, rapid shifts, overwhelming complexity, and constant pressure. In this kind of environment, the old model cracks. It's not a failure of individual capability, but a failure of a system that can no longer sustain itself.

The Cost of Constant Output

When output becomes the sole focus of leadership, the consequences start to emerge:

- burnout rises
- focus slips
- communication gets reactive
- decision-making becomes narrow
- engagement drops

What initially boosted performance eventually begins to erode it. The typical response is to double down: work longer, move faster, push harder. This doesn't fix the problem; it accelerates the breakdown.

The Missing Element: Capacity

The real limit isn't effort; it's **capacity**.

The ability to:

- think clearly
- focus deeply
- communicate effectively
- lead consistently

If that capacity is depleted, performance can't be sustained. Strangely, most leadership frameworks still fail to account for this essential element.

A Fundamental Shift

This is why we need a new operating system for leadership.

It requires a foundational shift away from traditional metrics:

- From Output to **Capacity**
- From Urgency to **Clarity**
- From Control to **Awareness**
- From Effort to **Sustainability**

This shift doesn't compromise performance; it actually makes it stronger. Sustainable performance isn't achieved by applying more pressure; it's built through **alignment**.

Introducing the Balanced Leader

The Balanced Leader Model is built on a few core principles: how leaders operate is just as crucial as what they achieve, a leader's internal state fundamentally shapes external results, and sustainable systems consistently deliver better outcomes.

This integrated framework supports leadership by building:

- nervous system awareness
- sustainable productivity
- emotional intelligence
- purpose-driven leadership
- confidence through alignment
- authentic leadership presence

How to Use This Book

This book is meant to be a resource you use and revisit, allowing your leadership approach to evolve over time. Each section progresses from understanding the concepts to applying them in real life, and finally, to embodying them in your presence.

A Year-Long Leadership Journey

This material also forms the core curriculum for the TrueJoy@Work program—a year-long, structured development experience. The program is designed to move leadership development from the conceptual to the practical through monthly focus areas, guided implementation, reflection, and real-world application.

What This Book Offers

This isn't a guide about doing more. It is about learning to lead differently. It is about building the capacity for:

- clarity in complexity
- stability in pressure
- alignment in decision-making
- sustainability in performance

A Starting Point

As you begin this journey, hold this single question in mind:

The core question is no longer: How can I do more?

The core question is: How can I lead in a way that allows performance to be sustained?

Because ultimately, the future of leadership belongs to those who recognize that performance isn't just manufactured—it's **supported**.

PART I

THE MODERN LEADERSHIP CHALLENGE

Chapter 1

The Demand for More Than Productivity

For decades, success at work has been measured by one primary standard:

productivity.

More output.
Faster execution.
Greater efficiency.

Organizations have been designed around this principle — optimizing systems, processes, and performance to increase what can be produced in less time.

This model has driven growth, innovation, and progress. But it has also created something less visible. Something that is now becoming impossible to ignore.

The Cost of Constant Output

Today's workplace operates at a pace that was never meant to be sustained indefinitely.

Leaders and employees alike are navigating:

- **continuous communication**

Where the workday is no longer defined by clear start and stop points, but by a steady stream of messages, emails, and notifications. Even in moments meant for focus, attention is pulled outward — responding, checking, staying connected. The expectation to remain engaged never fully turns off.

- **increasing complexity**

Decisions are no longer simple or isolated. They involve more variables, more stakeholders, and more moving parts than before. What used to be straightforward now requires constant evaluation, adjustment, and coordination.

- **overlapping priorities**

Multiple initiatives move forward at the same time, each carrying its own level of urgency. Instead of clear sequencing, work stacks. When everything feels important, it becomes difficult to determine what actually matters most.

- **constant availability**

Responsiveness has become a standard of performance. There is an unspoken expectation to be reachable, to reply quickly, and to stay engaged — regardless of time, workload, or capacity.

The expectation isn't just to perform — but to perform continuously.

Without pause.

Without reset.

Without recalibration.

Over time, this is where a subtle but powerful shift begins. Work becomes less about meaningful contribution…

And more about maintaining momentum.

And when momentum becomes the goal, something important is lost:

Clarity.

Not all at once. But gradually. Decisions become more reactive than intentional.

Communication becomes shorter, more functional, less thoughtful. Focus is divided, rather than directed.

And while output may continue…

The quality of how work is experienced — and executed — begins to change.

Because this is where the cost shows up. Not just in what gets done. But in how it gets done and who people become while doing it.

When Productivity Becomes Unsustainable

At first, the signs are easy to dismiss.

A little more fatigue.
A little less focus.
A slightly shorter attention span.

But over time, these small shifts compound.

Leaders begin to notice:

- decisions taking longer
- conversations becoming more reactive
- creativity declining
- teams feeling more strained

The issue is not a lack of capability.

It is a mismatch between what is being asked and what can be sustained.

Because productivity, when disconnected from human capacity, becomes unstable.

The Hidden Driver of Performance

What is often overlooked in conversations about productivity is the role of human energy. Performance is rarely limited by time alone. Most people have enough time to complete their work.

What they don't always have… is the capacity to use that time effectively. Because performance is not just driven by time, effort, or strategy. Those matter.

But they are not the full picture. Performance is driven by something less visible — and far more influential. Human capacity.

The ability to think clearly, stay focused, and engage with the work in a meaningful way depends on several underlying factors. It depends on cognitive capacity — the ability to process information, solve problems, and maintain attention without becoming overwhelmed. It is shaped by emotional state — whether someone feels steady, reactive, clear, or under pressure.

It is influenced by physical energy — the level of fatigue or alertness that directly affects focus and endurance. It's regulated by the nervous system — which determines whether someone is operating from a state of clarity and presence… or urgency and reactivity.

These elements are always present. Whether they are acknowledged or not. When they are supported, performance feels different.

Work becomes clearer. Focus is easier to sustain. Decisions feel more intentional. Tasks are completed with less friction.

There is a sense of efficiency — not because more is being done, but because less energy is being wasted. But when these elements are depleted, the experience of work changes.

Attention becomes harder to maintain, Responses become quicker, but less thoughtful. Effort increases, while clarity decreases.

Performance doesn't stop. But it becomes more reactive. More inconsistent. More effortful.

Over time, that difference compounds. This is why two hours of focused, intentional work can often produce more meaningful results than an entire day of fragmented effort.

Not because more time was available. But because the capacity to use that time was fully present. Because this is the work.

The Pressure Paradox

Many organizations respond to declining performance by increasing pressure.

More accountability.
More urgency.
More expectations.

And in the short term, this can work.

Deadlines are met.
Output increases.
Results appear.

But beneath the surface, something else is happening.

Pressure narrows attention. It reduces long-term thinking. It increases reactivity.

Over time, it erodes the very capacities that support sustained performance.

This is where a paradox:

The more pressure applied, the less sustainable the performance becomes.

The Shift Leaders Are Beginning to See

Forward-thinking organizations are beginning to recognize a critical truth:

Performance cannot be separated from the conditions that support it.

They are seeing that:

- focus requires uninterrupted space
- decision-making requires cognitive clarity
- communication requires emotional regulation
- performance requires recovery

This is not about lowering standards. It is about understanding what makes those standards achievable over time.

Beyond Output: A New Leadership Lens

The next evolution of leadership is not about abandoning productivity. It is about expanding how productivity is understood.

This includes shifting from:

Output → Capacity

Not just what gets done, but what can be sustained.

Urgency → Clarity

Not constant pressure, but clear direction.

Activity → Effectiveness

Not doing more but doing what matters.

Endurance → Sustainability

Not how long we can push, but how consistently we can perform.

This shift changes how leaders:

- make decisions
- structure work
- communicate expectations
- support their teams

What This Looks Like in Practice

When leaders begin to adopt this perspective, subtle but meaningful changes occur.

Meetings become more intentional.
Priorities become clearer.
Communication becomes more focused.
Teams experience less unnecessary pressure.

Work does not slow down. It becomes more **directed**.
As a result, performance often improves — not through force, but through alignment.

A More Useful Question

In traditional models, leaders often ask:

How do we get more done?

But in this new model, a more effective question emerges:

How do we create the conditions where meaningful work can happen consistently?

This question shifts leadership from pushing output to designing environments.

The Leadership Opportunity

Leaders today have an opportunity to redefine how performance is achieved. Not by removing expectations.
But by supporting the systems that make those expectations sustainable.

This includes:

- recognizing the limits of constant urgency
- creating space for focus
- supporting recovery and energy management
- modeling clarity instead of pressure

These are not soft skills. They are performance strategies.

Closing Reflection

The demand for productivity is not going away.

But the way we pursue it must evolve.

Because ultimately:

Performance is not just about how much is produced. It is about how consistently, effectively, and sustainably it can be maintained.

The leaders who understand this will not only achieve results. They will sustain them.

Workbook Reflection — Chapter 1

1. Where do you currently see pressure showing up in your work environment?

2. How does constant urgency impact your focus, decision-making, or communication?

3. What would change if clarity replaced urgency in your leadership approach?

4. What is one shift you could make this week to support more sustainable performance?

Chapter 2

The Biology of Burnout

Burnout is often described as an emotional state.

Exhaustion.
Disengagement.
Overwhelm.

But burnout is not just emotional. It is **biological**.

Understanding Burnout Beyond the Surface

In many workplaces, burnout is treated as a personal issue.

Something to be managed through:

- time off
- better boundaries
- improved mindset

While these can help, they do not address the full picture. Because burnout is not simply the result of working too much. It is the result of **prolonged stress without adequate recovery**. At its core, burnout reflects a system that has been under sustained pressure for too long.

The Nervous System Under Chronic Stress

The human nervous system is designed for cycles.

Activation.
Recovery.
Activation.
Recovery.

This rhythm allows the body to handle stress when needed and return to balance afterward.

But in many modern work environments, this cycle is disrupted.

Instead of moving between activation and recovery, individuals remain in a **prolonged state of activation**.

Constant deadlines.
Continuous communication.
Persistent expectations.

The nervous system begins to interpret this as ongoing demand — or threat. Over time, it adapts. But not in a way that supports performance.

What Happens in the Body

When stress becomes chronic, the body doesn't simply "push through." It adapts.

But not in a way that supports long-term performance. Several physiological changes begin to take place — often gradually, and often without being immediately recognized.

Cortisol levels remain elevated, keeping the body in a sustained stress response rather than allowing it to return to baseline.

The system stays in a heightened state of alertness, as if something urgent is always happening — even when there is no immediate threat. Rest becomes less restorative.

Sleep may still happen, but it doesn't fully replenish. There is less recovery between days, and the body begins to carry fatigue forward instead of releasing it.

At the same time, mental clarity begins to decline. Thinking becomes less precise. Focus becomes harder to sustain. Decisions require more effort than they should.

These shifts don't always feel dramatic. But they are consistent. Over time, they lead to noticeable changes in how people work and respond.

Focus decreases, making it harder to stay with a task without distraction. Fatigue increases, even when the workload hasn't changed significantly. Emotional reactivity becomes more common — responses happen faster, with less space to pause or consider.

Resilience begins to decline. Challenges that once felt manageable begin to feel heavier. The system is no longer operating from a place of capacity.

It's operating from a place of conservation. Eventually, the body begins to protect itself. Energy is reduced, engagement decreases, and efficiency drops.

Not because effort is lacking. But because the system is trying to sustain itself under continuous demand. When that happens, performance is no longer supported in the way it once was. Because this is the work.

The Shift from Overdrive to Shutdown

Burnout is not just about being overwhelmed. It often includes a shift from **overdrive to depletion**.

At first, individuals may push harder:

- working longer hours
- taking on more responsibility
- staying constantly engaged

But as energy declines, a different pattern can emerge:

- disengagement
- reduced motivation

- difficulty concentrating
- emotional withdrawal

This is not a lack of commitment. It is the body's attempt to protect itself.

Why High Performers Are Most at Risk

Burnout is particularly common among high performers. Not because they are less capable.

But because they are more willing to push through fatigue, override the body's signals of stress, and maintain high standards even under sustained pressure, they are often able to continue performing—at least for a time—despite conditions that are no longer supporting them.

Over time, this is where a pattern of sustained overextension. Without adequate recovery, even the most capable individuals reach a limit.

The Misconception of Resilience

Resilience is often framed as the ability to endure. To keep going despite pressure. But true resilience is not about constant endurance.

It is about the ability to:
- recover effectively
- adapt to stress
- maintain stability over time

Without recovery, resilience cannot be sustained.

Burnout as a System Signal

Burnout is not simply an individual issue. It is often a signal of systemic misalignment.

It can reflect:

- unclear priorities
- unrealistic workloads
- constant urgency
- lack of boundaries
- insufficient recovery time

Addressing burnout requires looking beyond the individual and examining the environment in which they are working.

The Leadership Role in Burnout Prevention

Leaders play a significant role in shaping the conditions that either contribute to or reduce burnout.

They influence:

- expectations around availability
- workload distribution
- communication patterns
- cultural norms

When leaders model constant urgency, teams often follow. When leaders model sustainable behavior, teams feel permission to do the same.

Reintroducing the Cycle of Recovery

To prevent burnout, organizations and individuals must restore the natural rhythm of:

effort and recovery.

This includes:

- creating space between demands
- allowing time for focused work
- supporting mental and emotional reset
- recognizing the limits of continuous output

Recovery is not a break from performance. It is part of performance.

What Sustainable Energy Looks Like

When the nervous system is supported, individuals experience:

- clearer thinking
- more stable focus
- improved emotional regulation
- greater adaptability

Performance becomes:

- more consistent
- less reactive
- more efficient

This is the foundation of sustainable leadership.

A More Useful Question

Instead of asking:

How do we prevent burnout?

A more effective question is:

> *What conditions are we creating that either*
> *support or deplete human energy?*

This shifts the focus from fixing individuals to improving systems.

Closing Reflection

Burnout is not a sign of weakness.

It is a signal.

A signal that the demands being placed on the system are exceeding what can be sustained. When that signal is understood — rather than ignored — it creates an opportunity.

An opportunity to design work differently. To lead differently. To create environments where performance and wellbeing support one another.

Because ultimately:

The most effective organizations are not those that push the hardest.
They are those that understand how to sustain energy over time.

Workbook Reflection — Chapter 2

1. Where do you notice signs of burnout — in yourself or your team?

2. What patterns of chronic stress are present in your work environment?

3. How does your current work rhythm support — or limit — recovery?

4. What is one change that could help reintroduce balance between effort and recovery?

Chapter 3

Why Focus Is Failing

Focus has become one of the most sought-after — and most elusive — capacities in the modern workplace.

Leaders ask for it.
Organizations expect it.
Individuals strive for it.

Yet despite best efforts, focus continues to decline.

Tasks take longer.
Attention drifts.
Distractions increase.

The common assumption is:

people just need to be more disciplined.

But this assumption misses what is actually happening. Focus is not failing because people do not care. It is failing because the conditions required for focus are no longer present.

The Illusion of Willpower

For years, focus has been framed as a matter of effort.

If you want to concentrate, you simply need to:

- try harder
- eliminate distractions
- manage your time better

While these can help in the short term, they do not address the underlying issue. Because focus is not just a mental decision.

It is a **biological state**.

When that state is disrupted, willpower alone is not enough to restore it.

The Overloaded Nervous System

The nervous system plays a central role in attention.

When it is balanced, individuals can:

- concentrate deeply
- think clearly
- engage with complex tasks

But when it is overloaded, attention becomes fragmented.

Modern work environments often create this overload
through:

- constant digital communication
- rapid task switching
- ongoing pressure and urgency
- lack of recovery time

In this state, the brain prioritizes:

- immediate demands
- potential risks
- quick responses

Over sustained focus.

The Cost of Constant Interruption

Each time attention is interrupted, the brain must shift
context. This shift is not immediate. It requires time and
energy to refocus.

Over the course of a day, these interruptions
accumulate: emails, messages, meetings, and
notifications

What appears to be small disruptions becomes a
pattern of fragmented attention.

The result is:

- reduced efficiency

- increased errors
- longer completion times

A sense that work is constantly in motion — but not always progressing.

The Fragmentation of Attention

When attention is repeatedly divided, something deeper begins to shift. The ability to sustain focus begins to weaken.

Tasks are approached in shorter bursts, with less continuity between them. Thinking becomes more reactive, shaped by what is most immediate rather than what is most important. Depth is gradually replaced by speed.

Over time, this shows up in subtle but meaningful ways. Complex problem-solving requires more effort than it once did. Sustained concentration becomes harder to maintain.

Completing meaningful work without distraction feels increasingly difficult. This isn't a lack of capability. It's a pattern that has been trained — through repetition, interruption, and constant demand.

The Role of Clarity

Another factor contributing to declining focus is lack of clarity.

When priorities are unclear:

- attention is divided across multiple tasks
- decision-making becomes slower
- effort is spread too thin

Clarity reduces cognitive load.

It allows individuals to direct attention toward what matters most — without constant re-evaluation. Without clarity, even the most capable individuals struggle to focus.

The Productivity Trap

In many workplaces, activity is mistaken for productivity.

Responding quickly.
Attending meetings.
Staying constantly engaged.

These behaviors create the appearance of effectiveness.

But they often come at the cost of:

- deep thinking

- strategic work
- meaningful progress

True productivity requires focus. And focus requires conditions that support it.

Rebuilding the Conditions for Focus

If focus is declining due to environmental and physiological factors, then improving focus requires changing those conditions.

This includes:

Reducing Unnecessary Inputs

Limiting interruptions and non-essential communication.

Creating Protected Time

Allowing uninterrupted periods for deep work.

Clarifying Priorities

Defining what matters most to reduce cognitive load.

Supporting Recovery

Providing space for mental reset between tasks. These are not complex interventions. But they require intentional leadership.

The Leadership Responsibility

Leaders play a critical role in shaping attention within their teams.

They influence:
- how time is structured
- how communication is managed
- how priorities are defined
- how urgency is applied

A leader who creates constant interruption trains distraction. A leader who creates clarity and space supports focus. Over time, this becomes part of the culture.

Focus as a Strategic Advantage

Organizations that understand how to support focus gain a significant advantage.

They are able to:
- complete work more efficiently
- improve decision quality

- increase innovation
- reduce unnecessary effort

Not by working harder. But by working with greater clarity and intention.

A More Useful Question

Instead of asking:

> *Why can't people focus?*

A more effective question is:

> *What conditions are preventing focus from happening?*

This shifts the responsibility from the individual to the system.

Closing Reflection

Focus is not a rare skill. It is a natural capacity. But like any capacity, it depends on the conditions that support it.

When those conditions are disrupted, focus declines. When they are restored, focus returns. Because ultimately:

**People do not need to be pushed to focus.
They need to be supported in accessing it.**

Workbook Reflection — Chapter 3

1. What are the most common interruptions in your workday?

2. How does constant task-switching affect your focus and efficiency?

3. Where is lack of clarity contributing to divided attention?

4. What is one change you can make to protect focused work time this week?

Chapter 4

Communication Under Pressure

Communication is one of the most essential — and most misunderstood — aspects of leadership.

It is often treated as a skill:

- something to improve
- something to refine
- something to manage

While skill matters, communication is shaped by something deeper.

State.

How we communicate is influenced not just by what we know, but by how we feel — especially under pressure.

When Pressure Enters the Conversation

In calm environments, communication tends to be: thoughtful, clear, and intentional

People listen.
They respond.
They collaborate.

But when pressure increases, something shifts.

Deadlines tighten.
Expectations rise.
Uncertainty grows.

And with it, the nervous system responds.

The Stress Response in Communication

Under pressure, the brain moves into a more reactive state.

This affects communication in several ways:

- listening becomes limited
- responses become quicker and less considered
- tone becomes sharper or more direct
- assumptions increase

Conversations that might otherwise be productive can become strained. Not because of the content —
but because of the **state behind it**.

The Breakdown of Listening

Listening is one of the first capacities to be affected by stress.

When the nervous system is activated:

- attention narrows
- focus shifts inward
- the mind begins preparing a response before the other person has finished speaking

This is where a gap. Words are heard, but not fully processed. Meaning is missed and communication begins to fragment.

Tone and Interpretation

Tone carries more weight than words.

Under pressure, even neutral language can feel:

- abrupt
- dismissive
- critical

This is because tone is interpreted through emotional context. When individuals are already under stress, they are more sensitive to perceived shifts in tone. A slight change in pace or delivery can be interpreted as tension — even when that was not the intention.

The Role of Assumptions

As pressure increases, the brain looks for efficiency. It begins to fill in gaps quickly — not always accurately, but fast enough to keep things moving. Over time, this creates a subtle shift in how information is processed

Assumptions begin to form about intent, often without full context. Conclusions are drawn before all the information is available. Curiosity decreases, replaced by a need to respond quickly.

These patterns don't feel obvious in the moment. But they change how communication is experienced. Assumptions can accelerate misunderstandings

Once they are formed, they tend to stick — shaping interpretation, influencing responses, and becoming increasingly difficult to reverse.

Why Communication Skills Alone Are Not Enough

Organizations often respond to communication challenges by introducing frameworks:

- feedback models
- structured conversations
- communication training

These tools are valuable. But under pressure, they are often not used effectively. Not because individuals lack understanding. But because the nervous system overrides the ability to apply them.

Without regulation:

- communication becomes automatic
- reactions replace responses
- clarity is lost

Regulation Before Communication

If communication is influenced by state, then improving communication requires addressing state first. Regulation is the ability to bring the nervous system back to a more balanced, responsive condition. It creates space between stimulus and response.

This space allows for:

- clearer thinking
- more intentional communication
- greater emotional awareness

Often, regulation begins with small actions:

- pausing before speaking
- slowing the pace of conversation
- taking a breath
- allowing silence

These shifts may seem minimal.

But they significantly impact how communication unfolds.

What Effective Communication Looks Like Under Pressure

When leaders communicate from a regulated state, conversations change.

They become:

- more focused
- more respectful
- more productive

Leaders are able to:

- listen fully
- ask clarifying questions
- respond thoughtfully
- maintain a steady tone

This does not remove pressure. It allows pressure to be navigated more effectively.

The Ripple Effect on Teams

Communication patterns don't stay contained to individuals. They spread.

Teams naturally begin to mirror the communication style of their leaders — not because they are told to, but because it becomes the norm they experience every day. When leaders communicate with urgency, teams begin to feel rushed, often prioritizing speed over clarity.

When communication carries tension, teams become more guarded, filtering what they say and how they say it. When communication is clear and steady, teams feel more confident, and interactions become more direct and effective.

Over time, these patterns don't just influence conversations. They shape the culture. Not through policy or intention alone…

But through repeated experience.

From Reaction to Response

One of the most significant shifts in leadership communication is moving from reaction to response.

Reaction is immediate.

Response is intentional.

Reaction is driven by pressure.

Response is guided by awareness.

This shift requires practice. But it is one of the most impactful changes a leader can make.

A More Useful Question

Instead of asking:

> *How can I communicate more effectively?*

A more effective question is:

> *What state am I in as I communicate —
> and how might that be influencing this
> interaction?*

This question shifts communication from technique to
awareness.

Closing Reflection

Communication is not just about what is said. It is
about how it is experienced. And that experience is
shaped by the state from which it is delivered. When
leaders learn to regulate first, and communicate
second, something changes. Conversations become
clearer. Misunderstandings decrease. Trust begins to
build.

Because ultimately:

**Effective communication does not begin with
words.**
It begins with presence.

Workbook Reflection — Chapter 4

1. How does pressure typically affect your communication style?

2. When do you notice yourself reacting instead of responding?

3. How does your tone change under stress?

4. What is one practice you can use to regulate before responding in conversations?

Chapter 5

The Confidence Illusion

Confidence is often seen as a defining trait of leadership.

Leaders are expected to:

- project certainty
- make decisions quickly
- communicate with authority

Confidence, in many environments, is associated with having answers.

Knowing what to do.
Predicting outcomes.
Moving forward without hesitation.

But in today's workplace, this model is increasingly difficult to sustain. Because certainty is no longer guaranteed.

The Changing Nature of Leadership

Modern leaders operate in environments defined by:

- rapid change
- incomplete information
- shifting priorities
- complex decision-making

In these conditions, waiting for certainty can lead to:

- delayed action
- missed opportunities
- reduced team confidence

Yet many leaders still feel pressure to appear certain — even when they are not. This is where a gap between internal experience and external expression.

The Illusion of Certainty

Certainty can create the appearance of control. It can reassure teams, simplify decisions, and provide a sense of direction.

But certainty is often temporary.

When leaders rely on it as the foundation of confidence, they may find themselves:

- second-guessing decisions when conditions change
- overcommitting to outcomes that are uncertain
- struggling to adapt when new information emerges

This is the illusion. Confidence becomes tied to something that cannot be consistently maintained.

The Pressure to Perform Confidence

In many organizations, leaders feel the need to:

- appear composed at all times
- provide immediate answers
- avoid showing uncertainty

This can lead to:

- over-analysis
- decision fatigue
- internal stress

Leaders may hesitate often not because they lack capability — but because they feel they must be certain before acting.

Over time, this pressure can limit effectiveness.

A Different Foundation for Confidence

If confidence cannot rely on certainty, it must come from somewhere else.

That foundation is **alignment**.

Alignment is the ability to understand what truly matters, make decisions grounded in those values, and move forward with clarity—even when outcomes are uncertain.

It creates a stable internal reference point.

One that does not depend on external predictability, but instead allows leaders to navigate changing conditions with greater consistency and confidence.

Confidence Through Alignment

When leaders are aligned:

- decisions become clearer
- communication becomes more consistent
- direction becomes more grounded

They do not need to know every outcome. They need to know how to decide.

Alignment allows leaders to:

- move forward without over-explaining
- adjust course without losing credibility
- remain steady in changing conditions

Confidence becomes less about certainty —
and more about **trusting the process of leadership**.

The Role of Self-Trust

At the core of aligned confidence is self-trust.

Self-trust is the ability to:

- rely on your judgment
- act without complete information
- adapt without self-doubt

It does not eliminate mistakes.

It allows leaders to move through them without losing stability.

Self-trust creates:

- faster decision-making
- clearer communication
- greater resilience

It is not about being right every time. It is about being able to navigate uncertainty with steadiness.

What Aligned Leadership Looks Like

Leaders who operate from alignment make decisions based on principles rather than pressure, allowing their choices to remain steady even when external demands shift.

They communicate direction clearly, even as outcomes evolve, creating consistency without needing to have everything fully resolved.

When situations change, they remain calm, adjusting without becoming reactive. When adjustments are needed, they take responsibility for them without defensiveness. Their confidence isn't performative. It's grounded — shaped by clarity, consistency, and trust in how they lead.

The Impact on Teams

Teams do not need leaders to be certain.

They need leaders to be:

- clear
- consistent
- trustworthy

When leaders demonstrate alignment:

- teams feel more stable

- communication becomes more effective
- trust increases

Confidence becomes shared — not forced.

Moving Beyond the Illusion

Letting go of certainty as the source of confidence can feel uncomfortable.

It requires:

- accepting ambiguity
- trusting internal judgment
- releasing the need to have all the answers

But it also creates space.

Space for:

- more adaptive leadership
- more thoughtful decision-making
- more authentic communication

A More Useful Question

Instead of asking:

> *Do I have enough information to be certain?*

A more effective question is:

> *Is this decision aligned with what matters
> most?*

This shifts confidence from prediction to clarity.

Closing Reflection

Confidence is not built by eliminating uncertainty. It is built by learning how to lead within it.

Because ultimately:

Certainty comes and goes.
Alignment remains.

Leaders who trust that alignment are able to move forward — with clarity, consistency, and confidence — even when the path ahead is not fully visible.

Workbook Reflection — Chapter 5

1. Where do you find yourself waiting for certainty before making decisions?

2. How does uncertainty affect your confidence or communication?

3. What values or principles guide your leadership decisions?

4. What is one decision you could approach from alignment rather than certainty?

A balanced leader understands that sustainable performance does not begin with strategy.

It begins with the body.

With awareness.

With regulation.

With the ability to maintain clarity under pressure.

We now begin building the core capacities that support focused, effective, and resilient leadership.

PART II

THE BALANCED LEADER FRAMEWORK

Chapter 6

Nervous System–Aware Leadership

Leadership is often understood through behavior.

How leaders communicate.
How they make decisions.
How they manage others.

But beneath behavior is something more fundamental.

State.

And state is shaped by the nervous system.

The Foundation Beneath Leadership

Before a leader speaks, responds, or makes a decision, the nervous system has already assessed the environment.

Is this safe?
Is this urgent?
Is this a threat?

This assessment happens automatically.

It influences:

- attention
- tone
- reaction speed
- decision-making

In other words, leadership does not begin with strategy.
It begins with physiology.

Why This Matters in Modern Work

Today's workplace places sustained demands on the
nervous system.

Leaders are navigating:

- constant communication
- ongoing pressure
- rapid change
- high expectations

Without awareness, this can lead to a state of
continuous activation.

In this state:

- responses become faster but less considered
- communication becomes more reactive
- clarity decreases
- emotional regulation becomes more difficult

Even highly skilled leaders can struggle — not because they lack capability, but because their nervous systems are overloaded.

The Difference Between Reaction and Response

One of the most important distinctions in leadership is the difference between reacting and responding.

Reaction is immediate.
It is driven by the nervous system's need to resolve pressure quickly.

Response is intentional.
It includes awareness, choice, and clarity.

When leaders operate from a reactive state:

- conversations escalate more quickly
- decisions are made with limited perspective
- misunderstandings increase

When leaders operate from a responsive state:

- communication becomes more thoughtful
- decisions are more aligned
- outcomes are more stable

The difference is not intelligence.

It is regulation.

Emotional Contagion in Leadership

Leadership is not contained within the individual.

It spreads.

Through tone.
Through pace.
Through presence.

This is often referred to as **emotional contagion**.

Teams tend to mirror the state of their leader.

If a leader is:

- rushed → the team feels pressure

- tense → the team becomes guarded

- grounded → the team becomes more stable

This influence is often subtle, but it is consistent. Over time, it shapes culture.

What Nervous System Awareness Looks Like

Nervous system–aware leadership is not about removing stress.

It is about recognizing how stress affects behavior and learning how to work with it.

This includes:

- noticing early signs of activation
- understanding personal stress patterns
- recognizing how state influences communication
- developing the ability to return to a grounded state

This awareness creates choice. Without awareness, responses are automatic. With awareness, leadership becomes intentional.

Regulation as a Leadership Skill

Regulation is the ability to bring the nervous system back to balance after activation. It's not about eliminating pressure. It's about expanding the capacity to lead within it.

Leaders who are regulated don't remove challenge — they respond to it differently. They pause before responding, allowing space between stimulus and reaction. Their tone remains steady, even when conditions are not. They are able to think more clearly under pressure, rather than being driven by it. And in doing so, they create space for others to slow down, process, and respond more effectively.

These behaviors are often interpreted as composure or presence. But they are not surface-level traits. They are rooted in physiology.

Simple Practices That Shift State

Nervous system regulation does not require complex techniques.

Often, small shifts create meaningful impact:

- slowing the pace of speech
- taking a breath before responding
- pausing instead of reacting immediately
- creating brief moments of stillness

These practices allow the nervous system to reset.

Even a small reset can change the direction of a conversation or decision.

From Individual Awareness to Cultural Impact

When leaders develop nervous system awareness, the effects extend beyond the individual.

Teams begin to:

- communicate more clearly
- respond more thoughtfully
- experience less unnecessary tension

Work environments become:

- more stable

- more focused
- more collaborative

This is how individual awareness becomes cultural change.

The Leadership Advantage

Leaders who understand their nervous system gain a significant advantage.

They are able to:

- navigate complexity with greater clarity
- manage pressure without becoming reactive
- support teams more effectively
- sustain performance over time

They do not eliminate stress.

They lead differently within it.

A More Useful Leadership Question

Instead of asking:

How do I handle pressure better?

A more effective question is:

What state am I in, and how is that shaping my leadership?

This question brings awareness to the foundation beneath behavior.

Closing Reflection

Leadership is not just what you do. It is how you show up while doing it. And how you show up is influenced by your nervous system.

When leaders begin to understand and work with this, something shifts. Reactivity becomes response. Pressure becomes manageable. Communication becomes clearer.

Because ultimately: **Leadership is not just communicated.
It is transmitted.**

And what is transmitted begins with state.

Workbook Reflection — Chapter 6

1. How do you typically respond under pressure — reaction or response?

2. What are your early signs of stress or nervous system activation?

3. How does your state influence your communication with others?

4. What is one small practice you can use to regulate before responding?

Chapter 7

The Physiology of Focus and Fatigue

In most workplaces, productivity is measured in time.

Hours worked.
Tasks completed.
Deadlines met.

But time alone does not determine performance.

What determines performance is something far more dynamic:

energy.

And more specifically, **cognitive energy**.

The Real Driver of Performance

Cognitive energy is the capacity required to:

- focus attention
- process information
- make decisions
- engage in complex thinking

It fluctuates throughout the day.

It is influenced by:

- sleep
- stress
- emotional state
- workload
- environment

When cognitive energy is high:

- work feels clear
- decisions come more easily
- attention is sustained

When cognitive energy is low:

- focus becomes fragmented
- simple tasks feel effortful
- decision-making slows

This is why the same task can feel easy at one moment and difficult at another.

Why Fatigue Is Misunderstood

Fatigue is often interpreted as a lack of motivation. But in most cases, it is not. Fatigue is a signal.

A signal that the system is:

- overstimulated
- under-recovered
- cognitively overloaded

When this signal is ignored, performance does not improve. It declines.

Leaders and professionals often attempt to push through fatigue. But pushing through does not restore energy. It depletes it further.

The Natural Cycle of Attention

The human brain is not designed for continuous concentration. It operates in cycles. Periods of focus are naturally followed by periods of decline. These cycles are essential.

They allow:

- mental reset
- cognitive recovery
- sustained performance over time

When these cycles are respected, focus can be maintained throughout the day. When they are ignored, fatigue accumulates.

The Impact of Continuous Demand

Modern work often disrupts these natural cycles.

Many professionals move from:

- meeting to meeting
- task to task
- message to message

Without pause. This is where a pattern of continuous demand without recovery.

Over time, this leads to:

- reduced attention span
- increased errors
- slower processing
- decreased creativity

The issue is not the amount of work. It is the lack of rhythm.

Attention as a Finite Resource

Attention is not unlimited. It is a resource that must be managed. Each task, decision, and interaction draws from this resource.

When attention is divided:

- focus weakens
- efficiency decreases
- mental strain increases

When attention is protected:

- work becomes more efficient
- thinking becomes clearer

- outcomes improve

Managing attention is one of the most important aspects of sustainable performance.

Sustainable Work Rhythms

High-performing individuals do not work continuously. They work rhythmically. Sustainable work rhythms include:

Focused Work Periods

Dedicated time for uninterrupted work.

Recovery Intervals

Short breaks that allow the nervous system to reset.

Transition Space

Time between tasks to reduce mental carryover.

Defined Endpoints

Clear stopping points that allow for closure and rest. These rhythms support both productivity and wellbeing.

The Role of Leaders in Energy Management

Leaders influence how energy is used within their teams.

They shape:

- meeting schedules
- expectations around responsiveness
- workload distribution
- norms around rest and recovery

When leaders prioritize constant activity, teams follow. When leaders prioritize sustainable rhythm, teams perform more effectively.

From Time Management to Energy Management

Traditional productivity focuses on time. But time is fixed. Energy is not.

Shifting from time management to energy management changes how work is approached.

It encourages:

- prioritization of high-value tasks
- intentional scheduling of focused work
- recognition of limits

- integration of recovery

This leads to more consistent performance.

What This Looks Like in Practice

Leaders who understand the physiology of focus and fatigue:

- schedule demanding work during high-energy periods
- reduce unnecessary interruptions
- allow space between tasks
- encourage breaks and recovery
- model sustainable work patterns

These actions create environments where individuals can perform at their best.

A More Useful Question

Instead of asking:

How can I get more done today?

A more effective question is:

How can I manage my energy so that what I do is clear, effective, and sustainable?

This shifts the focus from quantity to quality.

Closing Reflection

The future of performance will not be defined by how long people can work. It will be defined by how effectively they can use their energy.

Because ultimately:

Time is limited.
Energy determines how that time is used.

And leaders who understand this will create environments where both performance and wellbeing can thrive.

Workbook Reflection — Chapter 7

1. When during the day do you feel most focused and energized?

2. Where do you notice fatigue impacting your performance?

3. How often do you allow time for recovery between tasks?

4. What is one change you can make to support your energy and focus this week?

Chapter 8

Sustainable Productivity Systems

Understanding stress, focus, and energy is essential. But awareness alone is not enough.

Without structure, even the most insightful leaders fall back into reactive patterns, constant urgency, and fragmented attention

Sustainable performance requires more than intention.

It requires **systems**.

Why Traditional Productivity Systems Fall Short

Most productivity systems are designed for output.

They focus on:

- task completion
- time optimization
- efficiency

While useful, these systems often overlook something critical: **the human capacity required to sustain them.**

As a result, they can unintentionally reinforce:

- constant activity
- unrealistic workloads
- limited recovery

Over time, this leads to:

- burnout
- inconsistency
- decreased effectiveness

A system that ignores human capacity will eventually fail — regardless of how well it is designed.

Redefining Productivity

Sustainable productivity is not about doing more.

It is about doing what matters — in a way that can be maintained.

This requires a shift from:

activity → effectiveness

urgency → clarity

time → energy

This shift changes how work is structured.

The Core Elements of Sustainable Systems

Effective productivity systems support both performance and wellbeing.

They include four essential elements:

1. Clarity

Clarity reduces cognitive load.

When priorities are clear:

- decision-making becomes faster
- focus improves
- unnecessary work decreases

Clarity answers:

- What matters most?
- What can wait?
- What is no longer needed?

2. Structure

Structure creates consistency. It defines how work is organized and executed.

This includes:

- scheduling focused work
- setting boundaries around meetings
- creating predictable workflows

Structure reduces the need for constant decision-making.

3. Rhythm

Rhythm supports energy. It ensures that work is balanced with recovery.

Without rhythm:

- fatigue accumulates
- attention declines
- performance becomes inconsistent

With rhythm:

- energy is replenished
- focus is sustained
- output becomes more stable

4. Boundaries

Boundaries protect attention and energy.

They define:

- when work begins and ends
- when communication is expected
- when focus should not be interrupted

Without boundaries, systems become porous. When everything is urgent, nothing is prioritized effectively.

Designing Work That Supports Performance

Leaders have the ability to design work environments that either support or undermine productivity.

This includes decisions around:

Meetings

- Are they necessary?
- Do they have clear purpose and outcomes?
- Are they scheduled with space in between?

Communication

- Is responsiveness expected at all times?
- Are there guidelines for urgency?
- Is information organized clearly?

Workload

- Are expectations realistic?
- Is work distributed effectively?
- Are priorities aligned?

These design choices shape how work is experienced.

From Reactive to Intentional Work

Without systems, work becomes reactive.

Tasks are driven by:

- incoming requests
- immediate demands
- external pressure

With systems, work becomes intentional.

It is guided by:

- priorities
- planned focus
- structured workflows

This shift allows leaders and teams to:

- regain control of attention
- reduce unnecessary stress
- improve overall effectiveness

The Role of Leaders in System Design

Leaders are not just responsible for results. They are responsible for the systems that produce those results.

This includes:

- setting expectations
- modeling behavior
- defining priorities
- protecting focus

When leaders operate without structure, teams often follow.

When leaders implement sustainable systems, teams benefit.

Small Shifts, Significant Impact

Sustainable productivity does not require large-scale changes. Often, small adjustments create meaningful results: reducing one unnecessary meeting, clarifying top priorities for the week, protecting one block of focused work per day, and setting clearer communication expectations

These shifts accumulate over time. And as they do, they reshape how work is experienced.

What Sustainable Productivity Feels Like

When systems are aligned with human capacity, the experience of work begins to shift.

Focus becomes easier to sustain, rather than something that has to be forced. Reactivity decreases, creating more space for intentional thinking and clearer decisions. Work feels more manageable, even when demands remain high, because attention and energy are being used more effectively.

As a result, performance improves. Not through added pressure… But through alignment.

A More Useful Question

Instead of asking:

> *How can we get more done?*

A more effective question is:

> *What systems do we need to support consistent, high-quality work?*

This shifts the focus from effort to design.

Closing Reflection

Productivity is not just a function of effort. It is a function of structure. And when that structure supports clarity, rhythm, and boundaries, something changes.

Work becomes more sustainable. Teams become more effective. Leaders regain control of how performance is achieved.

Because ultimately:

The quality of work is shaped by the systems that support it.

Workbook Reflection — Chapter 8

1. Where do your current systems create unnecessary pressure or inefficiency?

2. How clear are your priorities on a daily or weekly basis?

3. Where could better structure improve your focus or workflow?

4. What boundary could you implement to better protect your time and energy?

Chapter 9

Emotional Intelligence as Leadership Infrastructure

Emotional intelligence is often described as a "soft skill."

Something useful.
Something supportive.
Something that enhances leadership.

But in today's workplace, emotional intelligence is not optional. It is foundational.

Beyond Skill: Emotional Intelligence as Infrastructure

Most leadership capabilities depend on emotional intelligence.

Communication.
Decision-making.
Conflict resolution.
Team engagement.

Without emotional intelligence, these areas become inconsistent. With it, they become more stable and effective.

This is why emotional intelligence is better understood not as a skill but as **infrastructure**. It supports everything else.

The Internal Layer of Leadership

Leadership is often evaluated based on external behavior.

What is said.
What is done.
What is achieved.

But these behaviors are influenced by an internal layer:

- emotional awareness
- self-regulation
- perception of others
- interpretation of situations

This internal layer determines how leaders respond — especially under pressure.

Self-Awareness: The Starting Point

Emotional intelligence begins with self-awareness.

The ability to recognize:

- thoughts
- emotions

- reactions

As they occur.

Without awareness, responses are automatic.

Leaders may:

- react defensively
- misinterpret situations
- communicate without intention

With awareness, leaders gain choice.

They can:

- pause
- adjust
- respond more effectively

Self-Regulation: Creating Stability

Awareness alone is not enough.

Leaders must also be able to regulate their responses.

Self-regulation is the ability to:

- manage emotional reactions
- maintain composure
- respond intentionally

Especially in challenging situations.

Without regulation:

- communication becomes reactive
- tension escalates
- decisions become less clear

With regulation:

- conversations remain productive
- pressure becomes manageable
- leadership presence is maintained

Social Awareness: Understanding Others

Emotional intelligence also includes the ability to understand others.

This involves:

- recognizing emotional cues
- understanding perspectives
- sensing shifts in tone and energy

Leaders with strong social awareness are better able to:

- anticipate concerns
- respond to team dynamics
- build stronger relationships

They are not just focused on tasks. They are aware of the human experience within those tasks.

Relational Intelligence: The Outcome

When self-awareness, regulation, and social awareness come together, they create something more integrated. Relational intelligence.

The ability to build trust through consistent behavior, navigate conflict without escalation, communicate with clarity, and support collaboration in a way that keeps teams aligned.

This is what allows teams to function well under pressure. Not because the pressure is removed…

But because the way people respond to each other remains steady, even within it.

Why Emotional Intelligence Breaks Down Under Stress

Even leaders with strong emotional intelligence can struggle under pressure.

This is because stress impacts:

- awareness
- patience
- perspective

The nervous system shifts into a more reactive state.

And in that state:

- listening decreases
- assumptions increase
- emotional responses intensify

This is why emotional intelligence must be supported by nervous system awareness. Without regulation, emotional intelligence becomes difficult to access.

Emotional Intelligence in Practice

Leaders who integrate emotional intelligence into their daily behavior:

- pause before responding
- ask questions instead of making assumptions
- listen without interrupting
- acknowledge emotions without overreacting
- respond with clarity and steadiness

These behaviors create environments where:

- communication improves
- trust increases
- teams collaborate more effectively

The Cultural Impact

Emotional intelligence does not stay at the individual level. It spreads.

Teams begin to:

- communicate more openly
- handle conflict more constructively
- support one another more effectively

Over time, this shapes culture. Not through policy but instead through interaction.

From Awareness to Consistency

The goal is not occasional emotional intelligence. It is consistent emotional intelligence.

This requires:

- ongoing self-awareness
- intentional regulation
- continuous reflection

Leadership becomes less reactive and more stable.

A More Useful Question

Instead of asking:

> *How do I improve my communication?*

A more effective question is:

> *What am I noticing internally, and how is it shaping my response?*

This shifts focus from behavior to awareness.

Closing Reflection

Emotional intelligence is not about being more expressive. It is about being more aware.

More aware of:

- internal state
- external dynamics
- the impact of both

And when this awareness is integrated into leadership, something changes. Communication becomes clearer. Relationships become stronger. Teams become more effective.

Because ultimately:

**Leadership is not just about what you do.
It is about how you relate.**

Workbook Reflection — Chapter 9

1. How aware are you of your emotional state during the workday?

2. What situations tend to trigger reactive responses?

3. How do you typically respond to emotional situations at work?

4. What is one way you can increase awareness before responding in interactions?

Chapter 10

Purpose as Strategic Orientation

In many organizations, purpose is treated as an abstract concept.

A statement.
A message.
A value displayed on a wall.

But purpose, when understood correctly, is not abstract.

It is **practical**.

It is directional.

And it plays a critical role in how leaders and teams make decisions, navigate uncertainty, and sustain performance.

Beyond Motivation

Purpose is often associated with motivation. Something that inspires people. Something that creates engagement.

While this is true, it is incomplete. Purpose is not just about feeling motivated. It is about having **orientation**.

An internal sense of direction that guides:

- decisions
- priorities
- behavior

Especially when external conditions are unclear.

Why Orientation Matters in Modern Work

Today's workplace is defined by constant change.

Leaders are required to make decisions:

- quickly
- with incomplete information
- under pressure

Without a clear point of orientation, decision-making becomes:

- reactive
- inconsistent
- influenced by urgency

Purpose provides a reference point.

It answers:

- Why does this matter?
- What are we working toward?
- What should guide our decisions?

With purpose, leaders are able to move forward with clarity — even when certainty is not available.

Purpose as a Decision-Making Framework

When purpose is integrated into leadership, it becomes a filter. A way to evaluate choices.

Instead of relying solely on:

- external pressure
- short-term outcomes
- immediate demands

Leaders can ask:

- Does this align with our direction?
- Does this support what we are building?
- Does this reflect what we value?

This reduces:

- decision fatigue
- inconsistency
- unnecessary complexity

Purpose simplifies.

The Connection Between Purpose and Performance

Purpose is not separate from performance. It enhances it.

When individuals understand how their work connects to a larger goal:

- focus improves
- engagement increases
- effort becomes more intentional

Work becomes more than a series of tasks. It becomes part of something meaningful. This does not require grand narratives. It requires clarity.

Purpose and Resilience

Purpose plays a meaningful role in resilience. When challenges arise — and they inevitably do — purpose provides a sense of stability.

It allows leaders and teams to navigate setbacks with perspective, maintain direction even when outcomes are uncertain, and recover more effectively when things don't go as planned.

Without purpose, challenges can feel disorienting.

With purpose, they become part of the process.

From Statement to Practice

Many organizations have purpose statements. But purpose only becomes effective when it is integrated into daily work.

This includes:

- aligning goals with purpose
- connecting individual roles to larger outcomes
- using purpose to guide decisions

When purpose is consistently applied, it becomes operational. Not just conceptual.

The Role of Leaders in Defining Purpose

Leaders play a key role in how purpose is experienced within organizations.

They influence:

- how clearly purpose is communicated
- how consistently it is applied
- how often it is referenced in decision-making

Purpose is not reinforced through repetition alone. It is reinforced through **alignment**.

When leaders make decisions that reflect purpose, it becomes credible.

Personal Purpose and Leadership

In addition to organizational purpose, leaders benefit from understanding their own sense of purpose.

This includes:

- personal values
- leadership intentions
- what they aim to contribute

When personal purpose aligns with organizational direction: leadership becomes more authentic, decisions become more consistent, communication becomes more grounded

This alignment strengthens leadership presence.

What Purpose Looks Like in Practice

Leaders who operate with clear purpose:

- communicate direction consistently
- make decisions with greater clarity
- reduce unnecessary complexity
- help teams understand the "why" behind the work

Teams, in turn:

- stay more focused
- collaborate more effectively
- feel more connected to outcomes

Purpose creates coherence.

A More Useful Question

Instead of asking:

> *What should we do next?*

A more effective question is:

> *What aligns with our purpose and direction?*

This question reduces noise and sharpens focus.

Closing Reflection

Purpose is not an abstract ideal. It is a practical tool.

One that supports:

- clarity
- decision-making
- resilience
- performance

When purpose is present, work becomes more aligned.
When it is absent, work becomes more reactive.

Because ultimately:

Purpose does not just inspire action.
It directs it.

Workbook Reflection — Chapter 10

1. How clear is your organization's purpose in your day-to-day work?

2. How often do you use purpose to guide decisions?

3. What personal values influence your leadership approach?

4. What is one way you can bring more alignment between purpose and action this week?

Chapter 11

Confidence Through Alignment

Confidence is often misunderstood in leadership. It is frequently associated with certainty, decisiveness, and outward assurance

Leaders are expected to appear confident — even in situations where outcomes are unclear. But in today's work environment, certainty is not always available. And when confidence depends on certainty, it becomes unstable.

The Limitation of Certainty-Based Confidence

Certainty provides a sense of control.

It allows leaders to:

- communicate direction
- make decisions quickly
- create reassurance

But certainty is often temporary. Conditions change. Information evolves. Unexpected challenges arise.

When confidence is built on certainty, it can be disrupted as soon as those conditions shift.

Over time, this leads to:

- hesitation
- second-guessing
- over-analysis

Confidence becomes fragile.

A More Stable Foundation

If confidence cannot rely on certainty, it must be built on something more stable. That foundation is alignment.

The connection between values, purpose, decisions, and actions — all working together rather than pulling in different directions. This creates internal consistency.

It's that consistency that supports confidence, even when outcomes are uncertain.

Clarity Without Complete Information

Leaders are often required to act without having the full picture. Waiting for complete information can delay progress. Aligned leaders approach this differently.

They do not wait for certainty. They rely on clarity.

Clarity comes from understanding:

- what matters most
- what direction to take
- how decisions align with values

This makes it possible to leaders to move forward with intention.

The Role of Self-Trust

At the core of alignment is self-trust.

Self-trust is the ability to:

- rely on your judgment
- make decisions without excessive validation
- adjust when needed without losing confidence

It is not about being right. It is about being able to navigate change without becoming destabilized.

Self-trust creates:

- steadiness
- adaptability
- resilience

Without it, leaders may hesitate or rely too heavily on external input.

Consistency as Confidence

Confidence is not always expressed through bold statements. Often, it is reflected in consistency.

Aligned leaders:

- communicate direction clearly
- make decisions that reflect their values
- follow through on commitments
- adjust when necessary, without losing focus

This consistency builds trust. And trust reinforces confidence — both for the leader and the team.

Confidence in Communication

Here's a refined version that keeps your tone but removes the outline feel and flows more naturally. When leaders operate from alignment, communication becomes clearer.

They speak with intention, choosing their words with more precision rather than over-explaining. They can acknowledge uncertainty without losing authority, creating space for honesty without creating doubt.

This is where an important balance begins to form. Between transparency and direction. Not sharing everything all at once…

But sharing what matters, in a way that keeps people informed and moving forward.

Teams do not require leaders to have all the answers. What they need is clarity.

Consistency.

A grounded presence they can rely on — especially when things are still evolving. Because this is where communication begins to build trust.

Navigating Uncertainty with Stability

Uncertainty is not something leaders can eliminate. It is something they must learn to navigate.

Aligned confidence allows leaders to remain steady even when outcomes are unclear. It gives them the ability to adapt without losing direction, and to support their teams through change without transferring unnecessary instability.

This is where stability begins to take shape. Not from controlling the environment…

But from how leaders show up within it — even when it is unpredictable.

The Impact on Teams

When leaders demonstrate confidence through alignment: decision-making becomes more efficient, communication becomes more trusted, and teams feel more secure

Confidence becomes shared. Not because leaders are certain —
but because they are consistent.

Moving from Performance to Authenticity

When confidence is based on certainty, it can become performative. Leaders may feel the need to appear certain, avoid showing uncertainty, and maintain a consistent image

When confidence is based on alignment, it becomes authentic. Leaders can acknowledge complexity, adjust direction, and communicate honestly Without losing credibility.

A More Useful Question

Instead of asking:

> *Do I have enough information to be confident?*

A more effective question is:

> *Is this aligned with what matters most?*

This shifts confidence from external validation to internal clarity.

Closing Reflection

Confidence is not created by eliminating uncertainty. It is created by learning how to lead within it.

When leaders are aligned:

- decisions become clearer
- communication becomes stronger
- direction becomes more consistent

Because ultimately:

Certainty is temporary.
Alignment is sustainable.

Leaders who build confidence on alignment create stability — not only for themselves, but for the teams they lead.

Workbook Reflection — Chapter 11

1. Where do you rely on certainty to feel confident in your leadership?

2. What values guide your decisions most consistently?

3. How does uncertainty affect your communication or decision-making?

4. What is one decision you can approach from alignment rather than certainty?

Leadership does not exist in isolation.

It shapes teams.

It influences culture.

It defines how people experience work.

As internal alignment strengthens, leadership begins to extend outward — into trust, communication, and collective performance.

PART III

CULTURE & COLLECTIVE IMPACT

Chapter 12

Psychological Safety Begins with Leadership Presence

Psychological safety has become a central focus in modern organizations. It is often described as the ability for individuals to speak openly, share ideas, admit mistakes, and challenge perspectives

Without fear of negative consequences. Organizations invest in policies, training programs, and cultural initiatives

All aimed at creating safer, more open environments. Yet despite these efforts, many teams still struggle. Because psychological safety is not created by structure alone.

It is created through **experience**.

And that experience is shaped, moment by moment, by leadership presence.

Trust Is Built Through Interaction

Trust is not established through statements. It is built through repeated interactions.

People continuously assess their environment by asking:

- Is it safe to speak honestly here?
- Will my perspective be respected?
- How are mistakes handled?

These questions are not answered once. They are answered over time — through behavior. Every interaction contributes to a pattern. Over time, that pattern becomes culture.

The Role of Leadership Presence

Leadership presence is not about authority. It is about how a leader shows up in moments that matter. This includes how they listen, they respond, they handle pressure, and how they engage with others

Presence influences whether people feel heard, whether ideas are shared, and whether challenges are addressed openly.

It sets the emotional tone of the environment.

Emotional Tone and Its Impact

Every team operates within an emotional tone. It's not always named, but it's felt.

At times, it may feel open and collaborative, where communication flows easily and ideas are shared without hesitation. In other moments, it can feel tense and reactive, with conversations becoming shorter and more guarded. Some environments carry a calm, focused energy, while others feel cautious — where people are more careful about what they say and how they engage.

This tone is not accidental. It is often shaped by leadership.

Leaders communicate tone through how they show up — through their pace, their body language, their responsiveness, and the consistency of their behavior over time.

Even small shifts matter. A steady, grounded presence creates space for others to think, speak, and engage more openly.

A reactive or rushed presence, even unintentionally, can create hesitation. And over time, those moments define how the team operates.

Behavior Defines What Is Safe

In moments of pressure, leadership behavior becomes especially significant.

When:

- someone challenges an idea
- a mistake is made
- difficult feedback is shared

Leaders signal what is acceptable.

If a leader:

- responds defensively → openness decreases
- dismisses input → contribution declines
- reacts with curiosity → engagement increases

These moments define the boundaries of psychological safety.

Why Policies Are Not Enough

Policies can encourage openness. They can outline expectations. But they cannot override experience.

If leadership behavior does not align with stated values, people will trust what they observe — not what is written. Psychological safety is not enforced. It is felt.

Presence as a Leadership Capacity

Presence is the ability to remain:

- attentive
- grounded
- non-reactive
- intentional

Especially in challenging situations.

It allows leaders to:

- listen fully
- respond thoughtfully
- hold space for different perspectives
- manage their own reactions

Presence creates stability. And stability supports trust.

What Psychological Safety Looks Like in Practice

In environments where psychological safety is present:

- ideas are shared more freely
- questions are asked without hesitation
- feedback is constructive
- mistakes are treated as opportunities to learn

This does not eliminate accountability. It strengthens it. Because people are more willing to engage, take responsibility, and contribute.

The Ripple Effect on Teams

When leaders consistently demonstrate presence, teams begin to mirror that behavior.

They:

- communicate more openly
- listen more effectively
- respond with greater awareness

Over time, this shapes:

- collaboration
- innovation
- performance

Psychological safety becomes embedded in the way the team operates.

The Leadership Responsibility

Psychological safety is not owned by a department.

It is created daily by leaders.

Through:

- how they show up
- how they communicate
- how they respond under pressure

Leaders do not need to be perfect. But they do need to be aware.

A More Useful Question

Instead of asking:

> *Do we have psychological safety in our team?*

A more effective question is:

> *What experience am I creating for others when they interact with me?*

This shifts the focus from concept to action.

Closing Reflection

Psychological safety is not something that can be implemented once. It is something that is built over time.

Through:

- consistency
- awareness
- presence

And when it is present, something shifts. Communication improves. Trust deepens. Teams become more effective.

Because ultimately:

People decide what is safe not by what is said — but by how it feels to be there.

Workbook Reflection — Chapter 12

1. How would you describe the emotional tone of your team or workplace?

2. How do you typically respond when someone challenges your perspective?

3. What behaviors contribute to trust in your interactions with others?

4. What is one way you can create a greater sense of safety in your leadership?

Chapter 13

Creating Trust-Centered Teams

Trust is often described as essential in the workplace and referenced in values. It is included in leadership principles and encouraged in team development.

Yet in practice, trust is not always present. Because trust is not created through intention alone. It is created through **consistency**.

What Trust Actually Means

Trust is not simply about liking or agreeing with others. It is about predictability. The ability to understand how someone will respond, what to expect from them, and whether their behavior aligns with their words

In a trust-centered environment, people know that they will be treated with respect, communication will be clear, and expectations will be consistent

This reduces uncertainty. And when uncertainty is reduced, collaboration improves.

Why Trust Matters for Performance

Trust is not just a cultural ideal. It is a performance driver. When trust is present communication becomes more efficient, decision-making improves, collaboration strengthens, and feedback is more effective.

When trust is absent information is withheld, communication becomes guarded, decisions are delayed, and conflict increases Trust affects how workflows through an organization.

The Role of Consistency

Trust is built through repeated, consistent behavior. Not occasional actions or isolated moments. But patterns over time.

Leaders build trust when they:

- follow through on commitments
- communicate clearly and consistently
- respond in predictable ways
- align actions with stated values

Inconsistency, even when unintentional, weakens trust. Because it introduces uncertainty.

Clarity as a Foundation of Trust

Clarity is one of the most overlooked elements of trust. When expectations are unclear people hesitate, assumptions increase, and misunderstandings occur

Clarity reduces:

- confusion
- unnecessary stress
- misalignment

Leaders who provide clarity:

- define priorities
- communicate expectations
- outline responsibilities

Create environments where trust can develop more easily.

Trust and Accountability

Trust and accountability are often seen as opposites. But they are interconnected.

In trust-centered teams:

- expectations are clear
- feedback is direct
- accountability is consistent

People are more willing to take responsibility when they trust the environment.

Because they believe:

- they will be treated fairly
- feedback will be constructive
- mistakes will be addressed appropriately

Trust does not remove accountability. It supports it.

The Impact of Leadership Behavior

Leaders influence trust through everyday behavior.

This includes:

- how they respond to challenges
- how they handle mistakes
- how they communicate under pressure

For example:

If a leader:

- reacts unpredictably → trust decreases
- avoids difficult conversations → trust weakens
- communicates inconsistently → trust erodes

If a leader:

- responds with steadiness → trust increases
- addresses issues directly → trust strengthens
- follows through consistently → trust builds

These behaviors accumulate. Over time, they define the level of trust within a team.

Repair as a Trust-Building Skill

Trust is not built through perfection It is built through repair. When misalignment occurs — and it will — leaders are given an opportunity. To acknowledge what happened, clarify what may have been misunderstood and to take responsibility for their role in it.

These moments matter. Because they strengthen trust. Not by avoiding mistakes. But by showing how they are handled.

Repair demonstrates accountability. It reflects awareness and it signals a clear commitment to realignment. Avoiding repair weakens trust.

Engaging in it reinforces it.

Trust and Communication

Trust improves communication.

When trust is present:

- people share information more openly
- feedback is more direct
- conversations are more productive

When trust is low:

- communication becomes filtered
- important information is withheld
- misunderstandings increase

Trust reduces friction.

Building Trust Over Time

Trust is not created quickly. It develops gradually.

Through:

- consistent behavior
- clear communication
- aligned actions

Small moments matter. Each interaction contributes to the overall experience.

What Trust-Centered Teams Look Like

In trust-centered teams:

- communication is open and clear
- expectations are understood
- feedback is constructive
- accountability is consistent
- collaboration is effective

Workflows more smoothly. Because people are not navigating uncertainty.

A More Useful Question

Instead of asking:

> *How do we build trust?*

A more effective question is:

> *What consistent behaviors are we demonstrating that allow trust to develop?*

This shifts the focus from concept to action.

Closing Reflection

Trust is not created through statements.

It is created through experience.

And that experience is shaped by:

- consistency
- clarity
- accountability
- behavior

When leaders understand this, trust becomes less abstract.

And more actionable.

Because ultimately:

**Trust is not built by what is said.
It is built by what is consistently done.**

Workbook Reflection — Chapter 13

1. How consistent is your behavior in communication and decision-making?

2. Where might inconsistency be creating uncertainty within your team?

3. How do you currently approach accountability and feedback?

4. What is one action you can take to strengthen trust this week

Chapter 14

Empowerment Without Chaos

Empowerment is often positioned as a goal in modern organizations.

Leaders are encouraged to:

- give teams more autonomy
- encourage ownership
- reduce micromanagement

And when done well, empowerment can lead to:

- increased engagement
- faster decision-making
- stronger performance

But when empowerment is not structured effectively, it can create something else: **confusion.**

The Misconception of Empowerment

Empowerment is sometimes misunderstood as stepping back. Giving space. Letting teams figure things out. Reducing oversight.

While autonomy is important, empowerment is not the absence of leadership. It is the presence of clarity, structure, and support.

Without these elements, autonomy becomes uncertainty.

When Empowerment Creates Chaos

When empowerment is introduced without clear guidance, teams may experience unclear expectations, inconsistent decision-making, overlapping responsibilities, and hesitation or overextension

This can lead to:

- reduced confidence
- slower progress
- increased frustration

The intention is empowerment. The result is misalignment.

The Balance Between Autonomy and Structure

Effective empowerment requires balance.

Too much control:

- limits initiative
- reduces engagement

- slows progress

Too little structure:

- creates confusion
- increases risk
- reduces accountability

The goal is not to choose one over the other. It is to integrate both.

The Role of Clarity in Empowerment

Clarity is the foundation of effective empowerment.

Leaders must define:

- goals
- priorities
- expectations
- decision boundaries

Clarity answers:

- What outcomes are expected?
- What decisions can be made independently?
- When should support be sought?

With clarity, autonomy becomes productive. Without it, autonomy becomes uncertain.

Decision-Making Boundaries

One of the most important elements of empowerment is defining decision-making boundaries.

Teams need to understand:

- what they can decide
- what requires approval
- where collaboration is needed

Clear boundaries:

- increase confidence
- reduce hesitation
- improve efficiency

They allow individuals to act without second-guessing.

Accountability as a Support Structure

Accountability is often viewed as restrictive. But in effective teams, accountability supports empowerment.

It provides:

- direction
- consistency
- feedback

When accountability is clear:

- expectations are understood

- progress can be measured
- adjustments can be made

Without accountability, empowerment loses structure.

The Leadership Role in Empowerment

Leaders do not step away in empowered environments. They shift their role. Instead of directing every action, they focus on guiding direction, supporting decision-making, and reinforcing alignment across the team.

This shift shows up in how they lead day to day. They provide context so decisions can be made with understanding. They clarify priorities so effort is directed where it matters most. And they offer feedback in a way that supports growth rather than control.

In this way, leaders are not removed from the work. They are creating the framework within which empowerment can succeed.

Trust and Empowerment

Empowerment is closely connected to trust.

Leaders must trust their teams to:

- make decisions
- take ownership
- learn from mistakes

At the same time, teams must trust leaders to:

- provide clarity
- offer support
- maintain consistency

This mutual trust strengthens both autonomy and accountability.

Learning Through Action

Empowerment includes the opportunity to learn.

This means allowing:

- decisions to be made
- mistakes to occur
- adjustments to follow

When leaders create space for learning:

- confidence increases
- capability grows

- teams become more resilient

Without this space, empowerment remains limited.

What Empowered Teams Look Like

In well-structured, empowered teams:

- roles and responsibilities are clear
- decision-making is efficient
- communication is aligned
- accountability is consistent
- individuals take ownership of outcomes

Work progresses with both independence and alignment.

Avoiding the Extremes

Leaders often move between two extremes:

Over-control

- excessive oversight
- limited autonomy
- reduced engagement

Under-structure

- lack of clarity

- inconsistent direction
- reduced accountability

Sustainable leadership exists between these extremes.
Where empowerment is supported by structure.

A More Useful Question

Instead of asking:

> *How do we give people more autonomy?*

A more effective question is:

> *What structure do we need to support
> effective autonomy?*

This reframes empowerment as a design challenge.

Closing Reflection

Empowerment is not about stepping back. It is about
stepping into a different kind of leadership.

One that provides:

- clarity
- structure
- support

While allowing individuals to:

- take ownership
- make decisions
- contribute fully

When these elements are aligned, something changes. Teams become more confident. Work becomes more efficient. Leadership becomes more effective.

Because ultimately: **Empowerment is not the absence of control. It is the presence of aligned structure.**

Workbook Reflection — Chapter 14

1. Where might a lack of clarity be limiting effective empowerment in your team?

2. How clearly are decision-making boundaries defined?

3. How do you currently balance autonomy and accountability?

4. What is one adjustment you can make to support more effective empowerment?

Chapter 15

Leading Through Change & Uncertainty

Change is no longer an occasional disruption. It is a constant.

Organizations today are navigating:

- evolving markets
- shifting priorities
- new technologies
- changing workforce expectations

For leaders, this means operating in environments where stability is not guaranteed. And where uncertainty is not temporary. It is ongoing.

The Nature of Uncertainty

Uncertainty creates discomfort.

It challenges:

- predictability
- control
- planning

When outcomes are unclear, leaders and teams may experience:

- hesitation
- anxiety
- increased pressure to find answers

In these moments, there is often a tendency to:

- move faster
- seek immediate resolution
- over-communicate or under-communicate

But reacting to uncertainty does not resolve it. It often amplifies it.

The Leadership Response to Change

In times of change, leadership becomes more visible. Not just through decisions. But through behavior.

Teams look to leaders for direction, stability, and clarity Even when clarity is limited. How leaders respond to uncertainty shapes how teams experience it.

From Control to Navigation

Traditional leadership often emphasizes control.

Planning.
Predicting.
Managing outcomes.

But in uncertain environments, control has limits.

Leaders are required to shift from controlling outcomes to **navigating complexity**.

This includes:

- adapting to new information
- adjusting direction as needed
- maintaining alignment without rigid certainty

Navigation requires flexibility. And clarity of purpose.

Clarity Without Certainty

One of the most important leadership capacities during change is the ability to provide clarity — even when certainty is not available.

This includes:

- defining what is known
- acknowledging what is not
- outlining next steps
- reinforcing direction

Clarity reduces confusion.

It allows teams to:

- move forward
- stay aligned

- maintain focus

Without clarity, uncertainty becomes disorienting.

The Role of Communication

Communication becomes especially important during change.

Leaders must balance:

- transparency
- direction
- consistency

This includes:

- sharing updates regularly
- avoiding unnecessary complexity
- reinforcing key priorities

Clear communication does not eliminate uncertainty.
But it reduces unnecessary stress.

Emotional Stability in Leadership

Change is not just operational. It is emotional.

Uncertainty can create:

- concern
- resistance
- fatigue

Leaders influence how these emotions are experienced.

Through:

- tone
- presence
- responsiveness

A steady leader can:

- reduce escalation
- create reassurance
- support team resilience

A reactive leader can unintentionally increase stress.

Supporting Team Resilience

Resilience is essential during change. But it is not created through pressure.

It is supported through:

- clear expectations
- consistent communication
- manageable workloads
- space for adjustment

Teams need time to:

- process change
- adapt to new conditions
- regain stability

Without this, change can feel overwhelming.

Flexibility Within Structure

Effective leadership during uncertainty requires both flexibility and structure.

Structure provides:

- direction
- consistency
- clarity

Flexibility allows for:

- adaptation
- responsiveness
- course correction

When these are balanced, teams are able to:

- move forward
- adjust as needed
- remain aligned

The Opportunity Within Change

While change can be challenging, it also creates opportunity. It allows organizations to rethink systems, improve processes, and strengthen leadership

Leaders who approach change with awareness and intention can guide teams more effectively, build trust, and create more resilient environments

A More Useful Question

Instead of asking:

How do we eliminate uncertainty?

A more effective question is:

How do we lead effectively within it?

This shift focus from control to capability.

Closing Reflection

Change is not something leaders can avoid. It is something they must navigate.

And how they navigate it shapes:

- team experience
- organizational effectiveness
- long-term performance

When leaders provide:

- clarity
- stability
- direction

Even in uncertain conditions, teams are able to move forward.

Because ultimately:

Leadership is not defined by certainty.
It is defined by how effectively you guide others
when certainty is not available.

Workbook Reflection — Chapter 15

1. How do you typically respond to uncertainty in your work?

2. How does your response influence your team?

3. What helps you maintain clarity during times of change?

4. What is one way you can support your team more effectively during uncertainty?

Understanding leadership is one level.

Applying it consistently is another.

But true leadership is revealed in embodiment — in how leaders show up in real time, especially under pressure.

This is where leadership becomes lived.

PART IV

EMBODIMENT & LEADERSHIP PRESENCE

Chapter 16

Calm Under Pressure

Pressure is a constant in leadership.

Deadlines.
Decisions.
Competing priorities.
Unexpected challenges.

Pressure is not the problem. How leaders respond to it
is.

The Misunderstanding of Calm

Calm is often misunderstood as passive.

Detached.
Uninvolved.
Slow.

But effective calm is not the absence of engagement. It
is the presence of **stability**.

A leader who is calm under pressure is not
disengaged. They are **regulated**.

What Happens Under Pressure

When pressure rises, the nervous system responds automatically.

The body prepares for action.

This can lead to:

- faster thinking
- quicker reactions
- increased urgency

In short bursts, this can be useful.

But when pressure becomes sustained, it can result in:

- reactive communication
- narrowed thinking
- reduced patience
- increased tension

Without awareness, leaders may operate from this state without realizing it.

The Difference Between Speed and Clarity

Under pressure, there is often a push toward speed.

Faster decisions.
Faster responses.
Faster execution.

But speed does not always produce clarity.

In fact, excessive speed can reduce accuracy, increase miscommunication, and create unnecessary work.
Calm creates space. And within that space, clarity becomes possible.

Calm as a Leadership Signal

Leadership is not only communicated through words. It is communicated through presence. A calm leader signals stability, control, and awareness

Even in high-pressure situations. This signal affects how teams respond.

When leaders remain calm:

- teams feel more grounded
- communication improves
- decision-making stabilizes

When leaders become reactive:

- urgency spreads
- tension increases
- clarity decreases

Calm is not contained. It is contagious.

Accessing Calm in Real Time

Calm is not something leaders either have or do not have. It is something that can be accessed.

Often through simple shifts:

- pausing before responding
- slowing the pace of speech
- taking a breath
- creating a moment of stillness

These actions allow the nervous system to reset. Even a brief reset can change how a situation unfolds.

Calm and Decision-Making

Calm supports better decisions.

It allows leaders to:

- identify multiple perspectives
- evaluate options more clearly

- respond rather than react

In high-pressure situations, this becomes especially important.

Because decisions made under reactivity often require correction.

Calm reduces the need for rework.

Maintaining Calm Without Suppression

Calm does not mean ignoring pressure. It does not mean suppressing emotion.

It means:

- recognizing what is happening
- staying present
- responding with intention

Leaders can acknowledge urgency without becoming consumed by it.

They can engage fully without becoming reactive.

The Practice of Calm

Calm is not developed in high-pressure moments alone.

It is built over time.

Through:

- awareness
- repetition
- intentional practice

Leaders who regularly create space for:

- reflection
- stillness
- reset

Are better able to access calm when it matters most.

The Impact on Teams

When leaders consistently demonstrate calm under pressure:

- communication becomes more measured
- teams feel more supported
- challenges are navigated more effectively

Calm does not remove pressure.

It changes how pressure is experienced.

Calm as a Leadership Advantage

In environments where urgency is constant, calm becomes a differentiator.

It allows leaders to:

- think more clearly
- communicate more effectively
- maintain direction
- support others

Calm is not a limitation. It is a strategic advantage.

A More Useful Question

Instead of asking:

How do I move faster under pressure?

A more effective question is:

How do I maintain clarity while navigating pressure?

This shifts focus from speed to effectiveness.

Closing Reflection

Pressure will always be part of leadership.

But reactivity does not have to be.

Leaders who learn to remain calm under pressure create something powerful.

They create:

- stability
- clarity
- trust

And in doing so, they influence how their teams experience even the most challenging moments.

Because ultimately:

Calm is not the absence of pressure.
It is the ability to lead effectively within it.

Workbook Reflection — Chapter 16

1. How do you typically respond when pressure increases?

2. What physical or emotional signals indicate
rising stress for you?

3. How does your response under pressure affect
your team?

4. What is one practice you can use to access calm
in high-pressure moments?

Chapter 17

Repair as Leadership Strength

Leadership is often associated with consistency.

Clarity.
Direction.
Stability.

And while consistency is important, leadership is not about perfection.

Misalignment will happen.

Conversations will miss the mark. Decisions will have unintended impact. Communication will sometimes fall short. The difference between effective and ineffective leadership is not the absence of these moments.

It is how they are handled.

What Is Repair

Repair is the process of restoring alignment after a moment of disconnection.

It includes:

- acknowledging what occurred
- taking responsibility when appropriate
- clarifying intention
- re-establishing trust

Repair is not about revisiting every detail. It is about addressing what matters.

Why Repair Is Often Avoided

Many leaders avoid repair. Not because they do not recognize its importance.

But because it can feel:

- uncomfortable
- vulnerable
- uncertain

There may be concerns about:

- appearing wrong
- losing authority
- creating additional tension

As a result, misalignment is often left unaddressed.

The Cost of Avoiding Repair

When repair does not occur, small moments accumulate.

Misunderstandings remain.
Tension lingers.
Assumptions form.

Over time, this can lead to:

- decreased trust
- reduced communication
- disengagement

What could have been resolved becomes embedded.

Repair Strengthens Trust

Contrary to common perception, repair does not weaken leadership.

It strengthens it.

When leaders engage in repair, they demonstrate:

- accountability
- awareness
- commitment to alignment

This builds trust.

Because it shows that:

- relationships matter
- communication is valued
- responsibility is taken seriously

Repair as a Leadership Signal

Just as behavior signals what is acceptable, repair signals what is important.

When leaders repair:

- it reinforces openness
- it normalizes accountability
- it encourages others to do the same

This is where a culture where:

- issues are addressed
- communication remains clear
- relationships are maintained

What Effective Repair Looks Like

Repair does not need to be complex.

It often includes:

- acknowledging the moment
- clarifying intention

- taking responsibility where needed
- expressing commitment to alignment

For example:

"I want to revisit our earlier conversation. I recognize that my response may have come across as abrupt. That was not my intention. I'd like to clarify and make sure we are aligned."

Simple, direct, and focused.

Timing Matters

Repair is most effective when it happens in a timely manner. Not immediately in heightened emotion. But not delayed indefinitely.

Creating space allows for reflection, clarity, and more thoughtful communication. But waiting too long allows misalignment to deepen.

Repair and Emotional Intelligence

Repair requires self-awareness, regulation, and willingness to take responsibility It is an extension of emotional intelligence.

Leaders who can recognize when something is off, how their behavior may have contributed, and what needs to be addressed are more effective in maintaining alignment.

Creating a Culture of Repair

When leaders model repair, teams begin to adopt the same approach.

They become more willing to:

- address misunderstandings
- clarify communication
- take responsibility

This reduces:

- unresolved tension
- communication breakdowns
- unnecessary conflict

Repair becomes part of how the team operates.

From Avoidance to Alignment

Avoiding repair may feel easier in the moment. But it often creates greater difficulty over time. Engaging in repair requires effort.

But it leads to:

- clearer communication

- stronger relationships
- more effective collaboration

It shifts teams from avoidance to alignment.

A More Useful Question

Instead of asking:

> *How do I avoid mistakes in leadership?*

A more effective question is:

> *How do I restore alignment when misalignment occurs?*

This reframes leadership from perfection to responsibility.

Closing Reflection

Leadership is not defined by getting everything right. It is defined by how leaders respond when things are not aligned. Repair is not a weakness.

It is a strength. A strength that builds trust, clarity, and resilience.

Because ultimately: **Trust is not built by avoiding missteps. It is built by how they are repaired.**

Workbook Reflection — Chapter 17

1. How do you typically respond when communication or alignment breaks down?

2. Where might you be avoiding repair in your leadership?

3. How comfortable are you with acknowledging misalignment or taking responsibility?

4. What is one situation where repair could strengthen trust right now?

Chapter 18

Integrating Mindfulness & Leadership Presence

Mindfulness is often associated with stillness.

Meditation.
Quiet environments.
Moments of reflection.

But leadership rarely happens in stillness.

It happens in:

- conversations
- decisions
- challenges
- movement

The question is not whether leaders can be mindful in quiet moments. It is whether they can be mindful **in motion**.

What Mindfulness Really Means in Leadership

Mindfulness is not about removing distractions.

It is about **awareness**.

Awareness of:

- internal state
- external dynamics
- how the two interact

In leadership, mindfulness becomes the ability to:

- stay present during conversations
- notice reactions before acting
- maintain awareness under pressure

It is not separate from leadership. It supports it.

Presence as a Leadership Capacity

Presence is the outward expression of mindfulness. It is how awareness is experienced by others.

A leader with presence is:

- attentive
- grounded
- engaged

Even in complex situations. Presence is not about doing more. It is about being **fully where you are**.

Why Presence Matters

In fast-paced environments, attention is often divided. Leaders may be thinking ahead, managing multiple priorities, and responding quickly

While this may increase speed, it often reduces connection, clarity, and effectiveness

Presence restores:

- focus
- listening
- intentional communication

It improves the quality of interaction.

The Link Between Mindfulness and Performance

Mindfulness is sometimes viewed as separate from performance. But it directly supports it.

When leaders are present:

- decisions are more thoughtful
- communication is clearer

- attention is more focused

This leads to:

- fewer errors
- more effective collaboration
- stronger outcomes

Mindfulness is not a pause from work. It is a way of improving how work is done.

Practicing Awareness in Real Time

Mindfulness in leadership does not require extended periods of stillness.

It can be practiced in small, consistent ways:

- noticing when attention drifts
- bringing focus back to the present moment
- observing reactions before responding
- listening without interruption

These moments build awareness. And over time, awareness becomes more accessible.

Managing Distraction

Distraction is one of the greatest challenges to presence. It comes from external inputs, internal thoughts, and competing priorities

Mindfulness helps leaders recognize distraction without becoming controlled by it.

Instead of reacting immediately, they can:

- pause
- refocus
- choose how to respond

This is where greater control over attention.

Presence in Communication

Presence significantly impacts communication.

When leaders are fully present:

- listening improves
- misunderstandings decrease
- conversations become more effective

People feel:

- heard
- respected
- understood

This strengthens relationships and trust.

Presence Under Pressure

Maintaining presence is most challenging — and most valuable — under pressure.

When pressure rises:

- attention narrows
- reactions increase
- awareness decreases

Mindfulness allows leaders to:

- notice these shifts
- regulate their response
- maintain clarity

This supports better outcomes in difficult situations.

From Awareness to Integration

The goal is not occasional mindfulness. It is integrated mindfulness.

Where awareness becomes part of:

- communication
- decision-making
- leadership behavior

This requires consistency. Small moments of awareness practiced repeatedly.

The Impact on Leadership

Leaders who integrate mindfulness and presence:

- communicate more effectively
- make more thoughtful decisions
- respond rather than react
- create more stable environments

Their leadership becomes:

- more intentional
- more consistent
- more effective

A More Useful Question

Instead of asking:

> *How do I manage everything more effectively?*

A more effective question is:

> *Where is my attention right now, and is it where it needs to be?*

This brings leadership back to the present moment.

Closing Reflection

Leadership happens in real time. Moment by moment.
And in each moment, there is a choice.

To react.
Or to respond.

To divide attention.
Or to focus it.

To operate automatically.
Or to lead with awareness.

Because ultimately:

**Presence is not something you add to leadership.
It is how leadership is experienced.**

Workbook Reflection — Chapter 18

1. How often do you feel fully present in your workday?

2. What most often pulls your attention away?

3\. How does distraction impact your communication or decision-making?

4\. What is one way you can practice presence in your daily leadership?

Chapter 19

Authentic Leadership in Action

Authentic leadership is often described as being genuine.

Being yourself.
Being transparent.
Being real.

While these ideas are important, authenticity in leadership is not simply about expression. It is about **alignment in action**.

Beyond the Concept of Authenticity

Authenticity is not a personality trait. It is not about how open or expressive a leader is.

It is about consistency between:

- values
- decisions
- communication
- behavior

When these elements align, leadership feels clear.

When they do not, leadership feels uncertain.

Why Authenticity Matters

In complex environments, teams are constantly interpreting leadership.

They are asking:

- Can I trust this direction?
- Is this consistent?
- Does this align with what has been said before?

Authenticity answers these questions. Not through words. But through behavior.

The Risk of Performative Leadership

When leaders feel pressure to meet expectations, authenticity can shift into performance.

Leaders may say what they believe is expected. They adopt styles that are not natural. They present certainty when it is not present

While this may create short-term alignment, it often leads to:

- inconsistency
- reduced trust
- internal strain

Teams sense when leadership is not fully aligned. Even if they cannot articulate why.

Authenticity as Alignment

Authentic leadership is not about revealing everything.

It is about ensuring that what is expressed aligns with what is true.

This includes:

- making decisions based on values
- communicating with clarity
- following through on commitments

Alignment creates consistency. And consistency builds trust.

Authenticity and Decision-Making

Authentic leaders make decisions that reflect:

- their values
- organizational direction
- long-term outcomes

They do not rely solely on:

- external pressure
- short-term reactions

- perceived expectations

This is where stability. Because decisions are grounded in something consistent.

Authenticity in Communication

Communication is one of the most visible expressions of authenticity. Authentic communication is clear, direct, and consistent.

It does not require over-explanation, unnecessary complexity, or constant adjustment Leaders are able to acknowledge uncertainty, provide direction, and maintain steadiness

Without losing credibility.

The Role of Self-Awareness

Authenticity requires self-awareness.

Leaders must understand:

- what they value
- how they respond
- where they may be misaligned

Without awareness, inconsistency can occur unintentionally.

With awareness, leaders can recognize misalignment, adjust, and realign behavior with intention

From Awareness to Action

Authenticity is not achieved through insight alone. It is expressed through action.

This includes:

- aligning behavior with values
- communicating consistently
- following through on commitments
- addressing misalignment when it occurs

Each action reinforces alignment.

Authenticity Under Pressure

Authenticity is most visible under pressure.

In these moments, leaders may:

- default to reactive behavior
- shift communication
- move away from values

Maintaining authenticity requires:

- awareness
- regulation

- intentional response

Leaders who remain aligned under pressure create trust.

The Impact on Teams

Authentic leadership creates:

- clarity
- consistency
- trust

Teams are able to:

- understand expectations
- align with direction
- engage more fully

Because they are not navigating inconsistency.

Authenticity and Leadership Presence

Authenticity strengthens presence.

When leaders are aligned:

- communication becomes more grounded
- decisions become more consistent

- interactions become more effective

Presence is no longer something that needs to be managed.

It becomes a natural expression of alignment.

A More Useful Question

Instead of asking:

How do I show up as a better leader?

A more effective question is:

Where might I be out of alignment between what I value and how I act?

This brings focus to the source of authenticity.

Closing Reflection

Authentic leadership is not about perfection. It is about alignment.

Alignment between:

- what is believed

- what is communicated
- what is done

When this alignment is present, leadership becomes:

- clearer
- more consistent
- more effective

Because ultimately:

Authenticity is not what you say about your leadership.
It is what others experience through it.

Workbook Reflection — Chapter 19

1. How aligned are your actions with your values in your leadership?

2. Where might you be adjusting your leadership style in ways that feel inconsistent?

3. How does pressure impact your ability to remain aligned?

4. What is one action you can take to strengthen alignment this week?

Leadership ultimately extends beyond results.

It shapes people.

It shapes culture.

It shapes what remains.

This final section explores leadership not just as performance — but as legacy.

PART V

LEGACY & TRANSFORMATION

Chapter 20

The Balanced Leader Model

Leadership is evolving. The expectations placed on leaders today are different than they were even a decade ago. Leaders are no longer responsible solely for results.

They are responsible for:

- how those results are achieved
- how teams experience the work
- how performance is sustained over time

This requires a new model. One that moves beyond intensity and endurance. One that integrates performance with sustainability.

The Limitation of Traditional Leadership Models

Traditional leadership models were built on control, efficiency, and output

These models assumed:

- stable environments
- predictable outcomes
- clearly defined roles

In that context, pushing harder often produced results.

But in today's environment — where complexity, change, and human demands are constant — this approach has limits.

Leaders may achieve results.

But at a cost:

- burnout
- disengagement
- inconsistent performance

The model works. Until it doesn't.

A New Definition of Leadership

The Balanced Leader Model expands how leadership is understood.

It is not about doing less.

It is about leading in a way that allows performance to be:

- consistent
- sustainable
- effective over time

It recognizes that performance is not separate from human capacity. It is dependent on it.

The Six Core Capacities of the Balanced Leader

The Balanced Leader Model is built on six integrated capacities. Together, they create a leadership approach that supports both results and wellbeing.

1. Nervous System Awareness

Leaders understand how stress affects decision-making, communication, and focus. They recognize their own patterns and develop the ability to regulate their state.

This makes it possible to them to:

- remain steady under pressure
- respond rather than react
- create stability for others

2. Sustainable Productivity

Leaders move beyond time-based productivity.

They manage:

- attention
- energy
- focus

They create systems that support:

- clarity
- rhythm

- boundaries

Over time, this leads to more effective and consistent performance.

3. Emotional Intelligence

Leaders develop awareness of their own emotional state and the dynamics of others.

They use this awareness to communicate more effectively, navigate conflict, and build stronger relationships

Emotional intelligence becomes a foundation for leadership behavior.

4. Purpose-Driven Leadership

Leaders operate with clear direction. They align decisions, priorities, and communication

With purpose.

This provides consistency, clarity, and focus Even in uncertain environments.

5. Confidence Through Alignment

Leaders build confidence not from certainty, but from alignment. They trust their decision-making. They act without needing complete information and maintain

consistency in changing conditions This is where
stability for both the leader and the team.

6. Authentic Leadership Presence

Leaders embody their values.

They:

- communicate clearly
- act consistently
- remain grounded

Their presence creates:

- trust
- clarity
- alignment

This is where leadership becomes fully integrated.

Integration Over Isolation

These capacities are not separate.

They are interconnected.

For example:

- nervous system awareness supports emotional intelligence
- purpose supports clarity in decision-making
- alignment supports confidence
- presence reinforces trust

The effectiveness of the model comes from integration.

Not from focusing on any one area in isolation.

From Pressure to Capacity

Traditional leadership often relies on pressure.

More urgency.
More demand.
More output.

The Balanced Leader Model shifts the focus to capacity.

Instead of asking:

- How do we get more from people?

It asks:

- How do we support people so they can perform consistently at a high level?

This changes how leaders:

- design work
- communicate expectations
- support teams

What This Looks Like in Practice

Leaders who operate from this model:

- create clarity instead of constant urgency
- protect focused work time
- communicate with steadiness
- respond rather than react
- align decisions with purpose

These behaviors may appear simple.

But they fundamentally change how work is experienced.

The Organizational Impact

Organizations that adopt the Balanced Leader Model begin to see:

- improved decision-making
- stronger communication
- higher engagement
- reduced burnout
- more consistent performance

Not because expectations are lowered. But because the conditions that support performance are strengthened.

A Model for the Future of Work

The future of work will require leaders who can:

- navigate complexity
- manage human energy
- lead with clarity and presence
- sustain performance over time

The Balanced Leader Model provides a framework for this.

It is not a trend. It is an evolution.

A More Useful Question

Instead of asking:

How do we increase performance?

A more effective question is:

How do we build the capacity that allows performance to be sustained?

This shifts leadership from output to foundation.

Closing Reflection

Leadership is no longer defined by how much can be produced in the short term.

It is defined by how effectively performance can be sustained over time.

The Balanced Leader understands that:

- performance and wellbeing are not separate
- clarity and presence drive effectiveness
- sustainable systems create better outcomes

Because ultimately:

**The future of leadership belongs to those who can balance performance with sustainability —
and lead in a way that allows both to thrive.**

Workbook Reflection — Chapter 20

1. Which of the six capacities feels strongest in your leadership today?

2. Which capacity would have the greatest impact if strengthened?

3. How do you currently balance performance and sustainability?

4. What is one step you can take to begin integrating this model into your leadership?

Chapter 21

Leadership as Stewardship

Leadership is often associated with ownership.

Owning outcomes.
Owning decisions.
Owning responsibility.

But there is another perspective that expands
leadership beyond ownership.

Stewardship.

From Ownership to Stewardship

Ownership focuses on control.

What is managed.
What is directed.
What is achieved.

Stewardship focuses on responsibility.

What is guided.
What is cared for.
What is sustained.

A steward does not simply lead for results.

They lead with an awareness of impact.

What Stewardship Means in Leadership

Stewardship is the understanding that leadership extends beyond immediate outcomes.

It includes:

- the experience of people
- the health of the organization
- the sustainability of performance

Leaders are not just responsible for what is produced.

They are responsible for how it is produced — and what it creates over time.

The Long-Term View of Leadership

Traditional leadership often prioritizes short-term results.

Meeting targets.
Achieving goals.
Driving performance.

While important, this perspective can overlook long-term impact.

Stewardship expands the time horizon.

It considers:

- sustainability
- consistency
- lasting outcomes

Leaders begin to ask:

- What are we building?
- What impact will this have over time?
- What will remain after this moment?

People as a Core Responsibility

At the center of stewardship are people.

Leaders influence:

- how people experience work
- how they grow
- how they perform

Stewardship includes:

- supporting development
- creating sustainable expectations
- fostering environments where individuals can thrive

People are not resources to be used. They are contributors to be supported.

The Environment Leaders Create

Leadership shapes environment. Through:

- expectations
- communication
- behavior
- systems

These elements determine whether an environment feels:

- supportive or demanding
- clear or confusing
- stable or reactive

Stewards take responsibility for the environments they create. They recognize that environment influences performance.

Sustainability as a Leadership Responsibility

Sustainability is often discussed in terms of systems or processes. But it is also a leadership responsibility.

Sustainable leadership considers:

- workload
- energy
- capacity
- long-term performance

It asks:

- Can this be maintained?
- Does this support ongoing effectiveness?
- What are the long-term implications?

Without sustainability, success becomes temporary.

Decision-Making Through a Stewardship Lens

Stewardship influences how decisions are made.

Leaders identify:

- immediate outcomes
- long-term impact
- effect on people
- alignment with purpose

This is where more balanced decision-making. Not slower. But more considered.

Integrity and Stewardship

Stewardship is closely connected to integrity.

Integrity is alignment between:

- values

- decisions
- actions

Stewardship ensures that leadership is not only effective but aligned.

This builds:

- trust
- credibility
- consistency

Over time.

The Ripple Effect of Leadership

Leadership does not stop with the individual.

It extends outward.

Through teams.
Through culture.
Through outcomes.

A steward understands that each action contributes to a larger system. And that system continues beyond any single moment.

From Short-Term Wins to Long-Term Impact

Short-term success can be achieved through pressure.

But long-term impact requires:

- alignment
- consistency
- sustainability

Stewardship prioritizes impact over immediacy. It ensures that what is built can last.

What Stewardship Looks Like in Practice

Leaders who operate as stewards:

- identify long-term implications of decisions
- support sustainable work practices
- prioritize clarity and alignment
- invest in people development
- maintain consistency in behavior

They lead with awareness of both present and future.

A More Useful Question

Instead of asking:

> *What do I need to achieve right now?*

A more effective question is:

> *What am I responsible for sustaining through my leadership?*

This expands the scope of leadership.

Closing Reflection

Leadership is not only about achieving outcomes. It is about shaping what those outcomes create. Stewardship brings a broader perspective.

One that considers:

- people
- systems
- sustainability
- long-term impact

And when leaders adopt this perspective, something shifts. Work becomes more intentional. Decisions become more aligned. Impact becomes more lasting.

Because ultimately:

Leadership is not just about what you build. It is about what you leave behind.

Workbook Reflection — Chapter 21

1. How do your leadership decisions impact others beyond immediate outcomes?

2. Where might short-term thinking be limiting long-term sustainability?

3. How do you currently support the growth and wellbeing of your team?

4. What is one way you can lead with greater stewardship this week?

Chapter 22

Embodying Leadership Legacy

Leadership is often measured by outcomes. Results achieved. Goals reached. Milestones completed.

But over time, something else becomes more significant. **Legacy.**

What Leadership Legacy Really Means

Legacy is not a final moment. It is not something that begins at the end of a career. Legacy is created continuously.

Through:

- decisions
- actions
- interactions
- presence

It is what remains in the experience of others.

Beyond Achievement

Achievement is visible.

Legacy is felt.

Leaders may be remembered for:

- what they accomplished

But they are experienced through:

- how they led
- how they communicated
- how they treated others

Legacy is shaped by:

- consistency
- integrity
- alignment

The Daily Expression of Legacy

Legacy is not built through occasional moments. It is built through everyday behavior.

Each interaction contributes to:

- how trust is formed
- how culture develops
- how people experience leadership

Small actions accumulate.

Over time, they define impact.

The Connection Between Presence and Legacy

Leadership presence plays a central role in legacy.

Presence influences:

- how others feel in your leadership
- how communication is received
- how trust is built

A leader who is:

- attentive
- grounded
- consistent

Creates a different experience than one who is:

- reactive
- inconsistent
- distracted

Legacy is shaped in these moments.

What People Remember

Over time, details fade.

But experience remains.

People remember:

- how they felt
- how they were treated
- how they were supported

This is the foundation of legacy. Not just what was said. But what was experienced.

Alignment and Legacy

Legacy is strengthened through alignment.

When leaders consistently align:

- values
- decisions
- behavior

They create:

- clarity
- trust
- consistency

Misalignment creates confusion.

Alignment creates impact.

Legacy and Leadership Responsibility

Leadership carries influence.

That influence extends beyond immediate outcomes.

It shapes:

- people's confidence
- team dynamics
- organizational culture

Leaders are not only responsible for results.

They are responsible for the experiences they create.

Intentional Leadership

Legacy becomes more powerful when it is intentional.

Leaders can ask:

- What do I want my leadership to represent?
- How do I want others to experience working with me?
- What impact do I want to leave?

These questions shift leadership from reactive to intentional.

Consistency Over Time

Legacy is not built through intensity. It is built through consistency. Repeated actions. Aligned behavior. Clear communication.

Over time, this is where:

- trust
- credibility
- lasting impact

The Role of Reflection

Reflection supports intentional leadership.

It allows leaders to:

- assess alignment
- identify patterns
- make adjustments

Without reflection, legacy is left to chance. With reflection, it becomes deliberate.

What Embodied Legacy Looks Like

Leaders who embody their legacy:

- act consistently with their values
- communicate with clarity and presence
- support others' growth
- maintain alignment under pressure
- create environments of trust

Their leadership is not defined by a single moment.

It is reflected in ongoing experience.

A More Useful Question

Instead of asking:

> *What do I want to achieve as a leader?*

A more effective question is:

> *How do I want to be experienced as a leader — consistently, over time?*

This brings legacy into the present.

Closing Reflection

Legacy is not something that is created later. It is created now. In each decision, each interaction, and in each moment of leadership.

And when leaders bring awareness to this, something changes.

Leadership becomes more intentional.
Behavior becomes more aligned.
Impact becomes more lasting.

Because ultimately:

Your leadership legacy is not what you leave behind. It is what others carry forward because of you.

Workbook Reflection — Chapter 22

1. How do you want others to experience your leadership?

2. Where is your current behavior aligned with that vision?

3. Where might there be misalignment?

4. What is one action you can take to embody your leadership legacy this week?

Chapter 23

The Journey of Transformation

Leadership is often approached as a destination.

A position to reach.
A level to achieve.
A role to fulfill.

But leadership is not a destination.

It is a **process**.

A continuous process of awareness, adjustment, and growth.

Beyond the Idea of Arrival

There is a common expectation in leadership:

That at some point, things become fully clear.
That confidence becomes constant.
That decisions become easy.
That uncertainty disappears.

But in reality, leadership does not arrive at a fixed state.

It evolves.

With each challenge.
With each decision.
With each experience.

Transformation Through Awareness

Throughout this journey, one element remains consistent:

awareness.

Awareness of:

- internal state
- external dynamics
- how the two influence one another

This awareness creates the ability to:

- adjust
- realign
- respond with intention

Without awareness, leadership becomes reactive. With awareness, leadership becomes adaptive.

Integration Over Information

Leadership development is often focused on learning.

New strategies.
New frameworks.
New tools.

But transformation does not come from information alone.

It comes from **integration**.

The ability to:

- apply what is understood
- embody what is learned
- practice consistently over time

Integration turns insight into action.

The Ongoing Nature of Growth

Growth in leadership is not linear.

There will be:

- moments of clarity
- moments of uncertainty
- periods of alignment
- periods of adjustment

This is not a sign of inconsistency.

It is part of the process.

Leaders who recognize this can remain steady, continue learning, and adapt without losing direction

Returning to the Core

Throughout this book, several core principles have emerged:

- awareness shapes behavior
- regulation supports clarity
- alignment creates confidence
- presence builds trust
- systems support performance

These are not steps to complete. They are capacities to develop and they are revisited continuously.

Leadership as Practice

Leadership is not something that is mastered once.

It is practiced.

In conversations.
In decisions.
In moments of pressure.

Each moment provides an opportunity to:

- respond instead of reacting
- align instead of adjusting to pressure
- lead with intention

Practice builds consistency. Consistency builds effectiveness.

The Impact of Consistent Leadership

Over time, consistent leadership creates:

- stronger relationships
- clearer communication
- more stable teams
- more sustainable performance

These outcomes are not achieved through isolated effort. They are built through repeated alignment.

Transformation at the Individual Level

As leaders develop these capacities, something shifts internally.

They become:

- more aware
- more steady
- more intentional

Decision-making becomes clearer. Communication becomes more effective. Leadership becomes more aligned.

Transformation at the Organizational Level

This shift does not remain at the individual level.

It extends outward.

Teams begin to:

- communicate more clearly
- collaborate more effectively
- operate with greater stability

Organizations become:

- more focused
- more adaptable
- more sustainable

This is how individual transformation leads to collective impact.

The Future of Leadership

The future of leadership will not be defined by:

- who can work the longest
- who can push the hardest
- who can maintain constant urgency

It will be defined by:

- who can maintain clarity under pressure
- who can support both people and performance
- who can lead in a way that is sustainable

This is the shift.

A Return to What Matters

At its core, leadership is not complex.

It returns to a few essential questions:

- How am I showing up?
- What am I reinforcing through my behavior?
- What experience am I creating for others?

These questions guide alignment.

A More Useful Perspective

Instead of asking:

When will I feel fully confident as a leader?

A more effective perspective is:

Leadership is not something to complete.

It is something to **continue**.

Closing Reflection

Transformation is not a single moment.

It is a series of moments.

Moments where leaders:

- pause instead of react
- choose clarity over urgency
- align with values instead of pressure
- lead with presence instead of habit

These moments accumulate.

And over time, they define leadership.

A Final Thought

The work of leadership is ongoing.

It requires:

- awareness
- intention
- consistency

But it also creates something meaningful.

Not just results.

But impact.

Because ultimately:

Leadership is not just about what you achieve. It is about who you become — and how that shapes everything around you.

Workbook Reflection — Chapter 23

1. What has shifted most in your understanding of leadership through this journey?

2. Which principle from this book do you want to integrate most consistently?

3. What does aligned leadership look like for you moving forward?

4. What is one commitment you are making as you continue this journey?

WORKBOOK APPENDIX

The Balanced Leader Integration Guide

How to Use This Workbook

This section is designed to support the integration of the leadership principles explored in this book. This workbook is designed to be revisited — not completed. Leadership is built through repetition, not perfection.

You can use it:

- individually for reflection
- with your team for discussion
- as part of leadership development programs

The goal is not perfection.

The goal is **awareness + consistent application**.

SECTION 1: STRESS & AWARENESS

Nervous System Awareness Check-In

1. What are your early signs of stress or pressure?

☐ Tightness in body

☐ Faster speech

☐ Shortened patience

☐ Difficulty focusing

☐ Other: _______________________________

2. What situations most commonly trigger stress for you?

3. How do you typically respond under pressure?

☐ React quickly

☐ Withdraw

☐ Over-control

☐ Stay steady

☐ Other: _______________________________

4. What helps you return to a more grounded state?

SECTION 2: FOCUS & PRODUCTIVITY

Focus Audit

1. What interrupts your focus most often?

☐ Email

☐ Messages

☐ Meetings

☐ Multitasking

☐ Other: _______________________________

2. How many uninterrupted focus blocks do you have per day?

☐ 0

☐ 1

☐ 2+

3. What is your highest-energy time of day?

Focus Planning Template

Top 3 Priorities for Today:

1.
2.
3.

Protected Focus Time:

Time Block: _________________________________

Distractions to Limit:

SECTION 3: COMMUNICATION & EMOTIONAL INTELLIGENCE

Communication Reflection

1. How do you typically communicate under pressure?

2. What patterns do you notice in your tone or responses?

3. Where could you listen more fully before responding?

Pause Practice

Before your next important conversation:

☐ Take one breath
☐ Slow your pace
☐ Focus fully on the other person
☐ Ask one clarifying question

SECTION 4: PURPOSE & ALIGNMENT

Leadership Alignment Exercise

1. What are your top 3 leadership values?

    1.
    2.
    3.

2. Where are you most aligned with these values?

3. Where might there be misalignment?

Decision Filter

Before making a decision, ask:

☐ Does this align with our purpose?
☐ Does this support long-term outcomes?
☐ Does this reflect my values?

SECTION 5: TRUST & TEAM CULTURE

Trust Builder Assessment

Rate 1–5:

Clarity in communication: 1 2 3 4 5
Consistency in behavior: 1 2 3 4 5
Follow-through on commitments: 1 2 3 4 5
Openness to feedback: 1 2 3 4 5

Where can trust be strengthened?

Repair Practice

Think of a recent misalignment:

What happened?

What needs to be acknowledged?

What would repair look like?

SECTION 6: ENERGY & SUSTAINABILITY

Energy Awareness

1. When do you feel most energized during the day?

2. When does your energy drop?

3. How often do you take breaks?
☐ Rarely
☐ Sometimes
☐ Consistently

Energy Reset Plan

One small reset practice I will implement:

☐ 5-minute break
☐ Walk
☐ Breathing
☐ Pause between meetings

Other: _______________________________

SECTION 7: THE BALANCED LEADER MODEL

Self-Assessment

Rate each 1–5:

Nervous System Awareness: 1 2 3 4 5
Sustainable Productivity: 1 2 3 4 5
Emotional Intelligence: 1 2 3 4 5
Purpose Alignment: 1 2 3 4 5
Confidence Through Alignment: 1 2 3 4 5
Leadership Presence: 1 2 3 4 5

Which area needs the most attention?

What is one action to improve it?

SECTION 8: WEEKLY INTEGRATION

Weekly Leadership Reflection

1. Where did I lead with clarity this week?

2. Where did I feel reactive instead of responsive?

3. What did I learn about my leadership this week?

4. What is one shift I will implement next week?

FINAL INTEGRATION PAGE

My Balanced Leader Commitment

I commit to leading with:

- ☐ Awareness
- ☐ Clarity
- ☐ Consistency
- ☐ Alignment
- ☐ Presence

One leadership shift I am committed to:

Signature: ___________________________________
Date: _______________________________

A Final Word

Leadership is not something you arrive at. It is something you practice. Not in perfect conditions.

Not when everything is clear. But in the moments that matter. In conversations, decisions, and in how you respond when things don't go as planned.

Throughout this journey, you have explored:

- awareness over reaction

- clarity over urgency

- alignment over certainty

- presence over performance

These are not ideas to remember. They are practices to return to. There will be moments when leadership feels steady.

And moments when it feels uncertain. This is not a setback. It is the process. What matters is not perfection.

What matters is your willingness to:

- pause

- realign

- respond with intention

- continue forward

Because leadership is not built in a single moment.

It is built in the moments you choose to show up differently.

Your Leadership Moving Forward

As you continue, consider:

- What kind of leader do you want to be —
  consistently?

- What experience do you want to create for
  others?

- What are you committed to sustaining, not just
  achieving?

These questions will guide you far beyond this book.

Continue the Journey

This book is part of a larger body of work.

The TrueJoy@Work experience is designed to support ongoing leadership transformation through:

- guided implementation

- structured reflection

- real-time application

- continued growth over time

Because leadership is not learned once. It is lived.

A Closing Reflection

Take a moment before you turn the page.

What is one commitment you are taking with you from this journey?

With Intention

Lead with awareness.

Lead with clarity.

Lead with presence.

And allow your leadership to create something that lasts.

Joy Hafner

TrueJoy Living

www.ingramcontent.com/pod-product-compliance
Lightning Source LLC
Chambersburg PA
CBHW050836060726
PP18531300001B/2